Moments, Attachment and Formations of Selfhood

DOI: 10.1057/9781137300577

Other Palgrave Pivot titles

G. Douglas Atkins: **T.S. Eliot Materialized: Literal Meaning and Embodied Truth**

Martin Barker: **Live To Your Local Cinema: The Remarkable Rise of Livecasting**

Michael Bennett: **Narrating the Past through Theatre: Four Crucial Texts**

Arthur Asa Berger: **Media, Myth, and Society**

Hamid Dabashi: **Being a Muslim in the World**

David Elliott: **Fukushima: Impacts and Implications**

Milton J. Esman: **The Emerging American Garrison State**

Steve Fuller: **Preparing for Life in Humanity 2.0**

Ioannis N. Grigoriadis: **Instilling Religion in Greek and Turkish Nationalism: A "Sacred Synthesis"**

Jonathan Hart: **Textual Imitation: Making and Seeing in Literature**

Akira Iriye: **Global and Transnational History: The Past, Present, and Future**

Mikael Klintman: **Citizen-Consumers and Evolutionary Theory: Reducing Environmental Harm through Our Social Motivation**

Helen Jefferson Lenskyj: **Gender Politics and the Olympic Industry**

Christos Lynteris: **The Spirit of Selflessness in Maoist China: Socialist Medicine and the New Man**

Ekpen James Omonbude: **Cross-border Oil and Gas Pipelines and the Role of the Transit Country: Economics, Challenges, and Solutions**

William F. Pinar: **Curriculum Studies in the United States: Present Circumstances, Intellectual Histories**

Henry Rosemont, Jr.: **A Reader's Companion to the Confucian *Analects***

Kazuhiko Togo (*editor*): **Japan and Reconciliation in Post-war Asia: The Murayama Statement and Its Implications**

Joel Wainwright: **Geopiracy: Oaxaca, Militant Empiricism, and Geographical Thought**

Kath Woodward: **Sporting Times**

DOI: 10.1057/9781137300577

palgrave▸pivot

Moments, Attachment and Formations of Selfhood: Dancing with Now

Kelly Forrest

Assistant Professor, University of Washington, Tacoma, USA

palgrave
macmillan

DOI: 10.1057/9781137300577

First published 2013 by
PALGRAVE MACMILLAN

Palgrave Macmillan in the UK is an imprint of Macmillan Publishers Limited, registered in England, company number 785998, of Houndmills, Basingstoke, Hampshire RG21 6XS.

Palgrave Macmillan in the US is a division of St Martin's Press LLC, 175 Fifth Avenue, New York, NY 10010.

Palgrave Macmillan is the global academic imprint of the above companies and has companies and representatives throughout the world.

Palgrave® and Macmillan® are registered trademarks in the United States, the United Kingdom, Europe and other countries.

ISBN: 978–1–137–30058–4 EPUB
ISBN: 978–1–137–30057–7 PDF
ISBN: 978-1–137–30056–0 Hardback

A catalogue record for this book is available from the British Library.

A catalog record for this book is available from the Library of Congress.

www.palgrave.com/pivot

DOI: 10.1057/9781137300577

To Peter

DOI: 10.1057/9781137300577

Contents

DOI: 10.1057/9781137300577

Acknowledgements

There are many people who have supported and guided me during the preparation of this book.

I am grateful to everyone in the Interdisciplinary Arts and Sciences program at the University of Washington, Tacoma for providing an academic home for interdisciplinary scholarship and supporting a quarter of research leave during the beginning stages of the Moments project.

For the UWT community of faculty, staff, students, and alumni who voluntarily agreed to share their moments, I would like to convey how honored and privileged I feel to be a witness to their level of transparency and trust. I hope my treatment of the moments conveys their wisdom.

I am grateful to my former students Jenn June and Daniel Pratt for their dedication and enthusiasm in assisting and doing all I asked of them at the start of the Moments project. To Rose Landberg, I remain in awe at the accuracy and timeliness with which she transcribed over a thousand pages of interview data.

I thank Mary Main and Erik Hesse, my trainers in the adult attachment interview; I have learned so much from their brilliant work. I also thank my colleague and friend, Paula Thomson for her insights on attachment and for providing a place to stay during the two weeks of intensive AAI training.

I have been encouraged and supported during this project by my sisters, Patti Turner and Gayle Rische, and my dear friends, Carolyn Mangelsdorf, Kathryn Kim, Martin Short, Helene Russell, Lauren Montgomery, Sally Fox, Steve Brown, Beth Kellner, and Victor Rigdon. How they meet the joys and struggles of daily life are a source of encouragement, inspiration, and guidance. In particular, I thank Barb Brant and Scott Brant for listening and responding so thoughtfully to my articulation of ideas and Nicki McGraw and Michael Culpepper for helping me understand how important sharing moments can be.

There are a few people without whom this book would never have existed or come to fruition. My wholehearted gratitude goes to Peter Thompson as the Moments project and this book developed and deepened through all the comings and goings, words and silences, sitting, walking, and running that I have shared with him. His presence and depth of humanity opened worlds I didn't know existed. As the project progressed, he read portions of the manuscript, offering suggestions and noting places that needed clarity. The *Dancing with* portion of the subtitle was fittingly inspired by his use of the phrase, and he and Ron Scharfe gave me the time and space to be in the Treehouse, where a majority of this book was written. My deep thanks also go to Chandan Reddy. He read portions of the book and ushered me through the process of finding a publisher. His intellectual generosity, joyful presence, and vision gave reality to a book I didn't know I had.

I thank Olivia Middleton at Palgrave Macmillan who believed in this project from the start and Nicola Jones and Harriet Barker who ushered the project forward. I also thank the team at Newgen Knowledge Works who guided me through the production process.

Lastly, I thank my animal friends, Maggie, Gracie, Koko, Canterberry, Connor, Kagan, and Annie for being with me.

DOI: 10.1057/9781137300577

Part I
The Journey

Abstract: *The reader is taken on a journey alongside the author's evolving relationship to the Moments project, an empirical study of the moments people remember from their lives. Moments are first introduced as a scholarly object of inquiry related to contemporary issues in the field of narrative identity. As the moments are collected and analyzed, however, a different relation to the moments emerges, a relation that explores the decontexted experience of moments, not as indicative of traumatic fragmentation, but as a normative phenomenon and a viable, although neglected, mode of healthy identity formation. Moments are viewed from their characteristic of having an inherent coherence in contrast to narrative meanings that are products of a construction process.*

Forrest, Kelly. *Moments, Attachment and Formations of Selfhood: Dancing with Now.* Basingstoke: Palgrave Macmillan, 2013. DOI: 10.1057/9781137300577.

Forty-four people, ages 18 to 61, shared up to three moments from their lives as part of a research project. Each person was affiliated with the University of Washington, Tacoma (UWT) community, as student, faculty, staff, and/or alumni. Their participation was voluntary. Moments were described as follows:

> We are studying moments that people remember as being important in their life and we are calling them moments that matter. A moment has a very short duration, up to about 10 seconds. You can think of a moment like a snapshot of experience. Moments that matter may be any type of experience. It could be a moment of realization, sharing something with someone, or sensing the warmth of the sun on your face. These are only examples, the moments that may come to mind for you may be similar to these or different from them. It may be a positive experience, a negative experience, or one that is neutral. What is important is that the moment comes to you when you think of moments that stand out for you, even if you don't know why.

We collected a total of 120 moments.

Why ask about moments? Certainly, we can remember salient moments from our lives, and it is kind of cool to think about those moments, but why research them? The first question I had was a phenomenological one, what are the moments people are remembering from their lives. The study of moments is growing, particularly in the therapeutic context, but in these studies, the types of moments have been pre-selected by researchers. Selected moments have included moments of misunderstanding (Rhodes et al., 1994), moments of sadness (Henretty et al., 2008), significant change moments (Helmeke and Sprenkle, 2000), problematic reaction points (Watson and Rennie, 1994), and helpful therapist interventions (Elliott et al., 1985). Outside the therapeutic context, the research is more sparse and diverse. As a sampling, pre-selected types of moments include moments of death (Donnelly and Michael, 2006), moments of wives' realization following husbands' diagnoses with HIV/AIDS (D'Cruz, 2003), "aha" moments in life-coaching (Longhurst, 2006), and moments of alienation in self-injurious behavior (Schoppmann, Schröck, and Schnepp, 2007).

Remarkably, though, no one has asked people in a research context what moments they remember from their lives, regardless of the type of moment. From all the experiences we have everyday, what will characterize the moments that people are remembering?

Moments tend to form around experiences that "break through the ordinariness or violate expected smooth functioning" carrying a sense

DOI: 10.1057/9781137300577

of consequence or engagement with the world (Stern, 2004, p. 34). Such moments are evident in the names they have been given, including a defining moment, a moment of truth, or a weird moment. Yet, moments can also be more ordinary, such as a moment of warmth on one's face, or realizing there is no butter in the refrigerator. Moments emerge spontaneously, coming into being as the moment is lived. They are formed implicitly, outside of awareness, but enter into conscious awareness.

This understanding of moments accords well with what is known about memory processes (for a review, see Siegel, 1999). Each lived experience has an initial impact on the brain, termed an engram. This engram links together various levels of experience: semantic (factual), autobiographical (your sense of yourself at the time), somatic (what your body felt like at the time), perceptual (what things looked like), emotional (your mood), and behavioral (what you were doing with your body). The first two types of experience are labeled explicit or declarative memory because they can be accessed in conscious awareness. Explicit semantic memory brings with it the subjective experience of recall or noetic awareness. Noetic awareness is characterized by knowing factual information, such as knowing that one took a trip to Europe last year. Explicit autobiographical recall adds the element of a sense of self in time or autonoetic awareness, such as recalling one's subjective experience of the trip. The remaining types of experience, such as perceptual or emotional, are termed implicit memory. When implicit memory is reactivated, it does not bring with it a sense of self, time, or that something is being recalled; it creates only the mental experience of perception or emotion. Such experiences are the foundation for a sense of self. The original experience includes linkages connecting each of the forms of explicit and implicit representation. Recall of an experience, however, is not just the reactivation of the associated elements of the original engram; rather, it is reconstructive, including features of the engram, together with elements from other experiences, and influences from one's present state of mind. Further, how an experience is recalled in the past affects how it will be recalled in the future because of the neural association that functionally links the activity of the neurons.

Research on the neuroscience of memory suggests that emotionally significant experiences create stronger, more durable memories (for a review, see McGaugh, 2003). But, what types of momentary experiences carry emotional significance? Will they be connected to significant life events, such as birth, death, marriage, or divorce? Will they be

DOI: 10.1057/9781137300577

experiences that challenge or transcend our ability to understand, such as mystical or religious experiences? Will they be characterized by moments of self-realization or mutual understanding, or connected to pivotal moments of change? Will there be moments that partake more of the everyday? Will the moments that people remember tend to be intersubjective, self-reflective, or perception-based, and will they be from an individual's recent or more distant past?

I was also interested in the extent to which moments are integrated into identity or a sense of self? Personal narratives have been tightly linked with the sense of self and the construction of identity (Giddens, 1991; McAdams, 1993). Would these shorter duration moments that people are remembering be part of personal stories or would some of them be left, like edited frames of a film, isolated and unstoried experiences? If so left, would they represent only incoherent fragments of traumatic experiences? There is considerable scholarship regarding the fragmentary nature of traumatic memory and I had questions whether non-traumatic memory might also be retained in memory without being integrated into a well-organized narrative.

One salient debate regarding the construction of self/identity in narrative is that of the relative contribution of the individual versus society (McAdams, Josselson, and Lieblich, 2006). The differing perspectives that exist in the narrative literature regarding this issue have been tentatively organized along a continuum (Smith and Sparkes, 2008). At one pole, there are theories that give more weight to the individual and relatively less weight to socio-cultural factors. Theories falling under this perspective are labeled interpersonal. At the other pole, there are theories, labeled performative, in which the self loses its individuality to a greater degree to the social-cultural-historical milieu in which it lives. At the midpoint between the poles is the intersubjective perspective wherein the self and the social/relational nature of the world carry equal weight in self/identity construction.

Thus, I was interested in the extent to which people were sharing their moments with others. If moments are reported to have an impact on self/identity construction and are not being shared as part of larger self-narratives, this would suggest a role for the individual in self/identity construction. It also raises the issue whether moments, given their shorter duration and focus on subjective phenomenal experience, partake more of raw experience and less from the socio-cultural discourses that are, to some relative degree, influencing our self-narratives.

DOI: 10.1057/9781137300577

A second debate in the narrative literature concerns the issue of unity or multiplicity of self (McAdams, Josselson, and Lieblich, 2006). Some theorists argue that life stories serve an integrative, unifying function, bringing different aspects of the self together into a coherent whole (Erikson, 1963; McAdams, 1985). Others assert contemporary social life is too complex and inconsistent to allow for an integrated identity and suggest that narratives are multivoiced, often including conflicting images of self (Hermans, 1996; Hermans, 2001).

If individuals have included remembered moments into their narratives, it would point to the attention people are giving to this integrative function, revealing an ongoing process of identity integration, as suggested by Erikson and McAdams. If moments conflict or are to some extent inconsistent with one's sense of self, then regardless of an integrating process that may be underway, the results would also provide support for viewing the self as a multiplicity (Hermans, 1996), at least at any given point within the lifespan.

These questions guided the construction of the interview in which each subject was asked to share up to three moments, the degree to which each moment had influenced their thinking, feeling, behavior, or their self, and whether their moments had been shared with others and in what contexts. Subjects were also asked which of the moments they remembered was most important, whether they discerned any relation between their moments, and what their experience was during the interview.

During the interviewing process, however, something different began to emerge, a different awareness, or better yet, a different relation to the project. The subjects in this study were sharing moments that, prior to that time, many had shared with only an intimate few, and some with no one else. At times, I felt like a voyeur, witnessing intimacies without the relational connection and depth that such sharing generally entails. I also began to feel oddly somewhat like a honeybee, going from human flower to human flower, receiving the essences of what had been culled from lifetimes of experience, a kind of human nectar.

The research project, or more accurately my relationship to the project, began to seem a bit coarse in relation to the intimacy and reality of the human experiencing I was being privileged to witness. I realized, after some time, that I was addressing an issue of ethics, of responsibility. How to be with these moments? How do I present them, order them, context their description to lessen, to the extent possible, the encounter with, what the Irish call, cold eyes, including my own? To what extent would

DOI: 10.1057/9781137300577

any such contexting or interpretation contribute to such an encounter? Academic scholarship has a tendency to veil lived experience within a web of discipline-specific language and theorizing while simultaneously, apparently, intending its revelation. I didn't want that for these moments; there was something about them that I didn't want to shroud with whatever critical apparatus I brought to bear to satisfy the requirements of scholarship, or at least my understanding of those requirements.

As I moved into analyzing the data, this feeling did not abate, but rather it broadened and deepened. I began to feel a kind of paralysis about how to move forward. Somehow this research was triggering something in me, something important, something underneath the conditioned layers of my academic training. It was something about what the moments were saying about how to live, something that was different from what I had been doing all my life.

To gain a sense of this, imagine, if you will, climbing up and standing atop a twenty-foot telephone pole. You can imagine footholds and being harnessed in if that helps, but what becomes increasingly salient as you settle both feet on the small flat surface that is the top and attempt to stand upright, is that you have nothing to hold onto. But, due to the increased field of vision from this viewpoint and perhaps some measure of pride for the climb, you think this really wouldn't be so difficult if the pole would just stop shaking.

Doubtless there are few of us who have actually had this literal experience, but doubtless also that few cannot relate to the feelings of uncertainty that arise when, for whatever reason, the ground beneath our feet begins to move. In a world in which mathematics has lost its certainties (Kline, 1980) and the histories and landscapes of our searching for understanding have led to global climate change, political polarities, genocides, financial bankruptcy, and countless endangered species, there seems little doubt that something is amiss.

In this metaphor, the pole represents our understanding of ourselves and the world. We stand at what always is the top and can look back or down to some major footholds within the history of meaning and value in western thought (for a review, see Angell and Helm, 1988). This is, of course, just another story, with all its flaws, gaps, and interpretations, but we will get to that a bit later.

In the late 1800's, we stood shaking our heads before the Michelson-Morley experiments that showed incredulously that the earth had no motion, that is, the earth was the anachronistic, Ptolemaic, stationary

DOI: 10.1057/9781137300577

center of the universe. With another step, with Einstein's general and special theories of relativity, we realized the earlier difficulty. There were no optical or mechanical experiments that any observer could perform to determine whether one is at rest or in uniform or accelerated motion (Angell and Helm, 1988, p. 452). The picture of the world under the visible ground was changing as well. Classical mechanics gave way to quantum mechanics as the view of solid subatomic particles changed to that of complex forms of energy. Heisenberg's principle of indeterminacy set the pole shaking at the submicroscopic level, leading scientists to rely on the statistical reliability found in the study of large groups, thus glossing over the minutest of shakings that only the severest of those with motion sickness might find problematic.

In philosophy, we have sought for stable ground as well, identifying universal ideals in the mind (idealism), holding fast to the physical nature of all substances (materialism), or discovering permanence in the relationships between things (structuralism). We have variously understood that sense data is immediately pressed on our minds (empiricism), that sense data is mediated by innate cognitive structures (rationalism), that the underlying innate structure is an economic one (Marx), or that everything has the structure of language (Saussure). We have retreated from dogma and sought meaning in the practical consequences resulting from any given idea and focused our attention on the production of results (pragmatism). We have reduced philosophy to logic and truth functions (realism-Russell), and have pruned philosophy to deny meaning to any language that could not be verified by the sciences or mathematics (logical positivism). We have shaken off the illusions of abstract systems to return focus to the self (existentialism) and hailed the discovery of meaning within the interplay of difference (poststructuralism). Currently, it appears, we are engaging our resources to excavate beneath our feet to ascertain how we construct the ground upon which we stand and interpret, explain, or transform it (critical theory).

Narrowing the focus to the social sciences, the views have ranged from the more materialistic/mechanistic, in which humans are little more than stimulus-response automatons (behaviorism) and consciousness is identical with brain states (neurosciences), to the more humanistic stances, which focus on the individual. We have understood ourselves as in some inherent conflict with others (Freud) or with ourselves (Jung), or rested the root of our conflicts on problematic childhood experiences (object-relations). Within this range, emphases have been lain on

DOI: 10.1057/9781137300577

a myriad of factors, including observables, the unconscious, creativity, and experience.

At this point, I am reminded of a summer three years ago sitting on the grass in the backyard of a friend. Connor, a 3-legged golden retriever and absolute lover of golf balls, is on his haunches chewing on one particular ball that looks as if it contains all possible delights. He is rolling the ball against the sides of his cheeks, chomping on it, maneuvering it with his tongue from side to side. He drops the ball from his mouth and braces it against his front leg and gnaws some more. He raises his neck to keep the ball from rolling forward beyond the reach of his paws. His breath keeps time with his jaw, in breath, jaw open, out breath, jaw closing, in, out, open, close. Then, he drops it in front of him and pants. He seems satisfied. Are we?

Perhaps, as many have suggested, we are searching for meaning. The motivations or sources of our searching have been thoughtfully categorized by Ford (2007). We seek orientation and identity through story (mythic mind), permanence and stability through form (philosophic mind), and predictability and control through an understanding of causation (scientific mind). We search for "a renewed sense of wonder in this world" (religious naturalism), "a timeless and universal basis for value and orientation" (metaphysics), or "a human universal source of meaning, identity, and stability" (archetypal psychology). We also seek to undermine "monolithic forms of thoughts and experiences" (postmodern mind) and to "accommodate pluralism and the limitations of intentional, instrumental thought" (pragmatism). We may or may not notice that the question of meaning arises from a position of separation between what is and what ought or could be, between meaning and meaninglessness, as the price we pay for self-consciousness (Ford, 2007).

It seems what is needed is some foundation that can move with each moment, but still serve as a foundation. Perhaps on the shifting seas of our thinking, we might build a boat? But, this metaphor quickly collapses. How do we create such a "structure?" Can there be only one structure? Is it a structure? Is it a state of body, of mind, of understanding the relations between each? Is it about understanding at all? Must each person find that space, state, center, process, experience, or context that allows a sense of equilibrium within the uncertainty? Or must this process be taken collectively, one with another? Is there one or are there many such spaces, states, centers...? How do we find the explanation

DOI: 10.1057/9781137300577

that replaces our uncertainty (Spence, 1982)? In every object that I see, in every thought I have, in every theory in which I find some truth, lives a grasping or rejecting of another object, another thought, another truth, another story. Do I use what I have learned, my experience, to shape or direct my future (Pillemer, 2003) and continuously revise my identity (Giddens, 1991)? But, if I use my past experience to guide my future, aren't I limited by that past? Isn't even the horizon of my imagination limited by that past? The field of narrative therapy is based on assisting with the limitations of such framings (Singer, Baddeley, and Frantsve, 2008). Yet, each moment brings new uncertainties. Are we not still left with the question of how – *how* to confront that which is in front of us? When I think of theories or stories, they remind me of dreams as Piaget (1954) speaks of the earliest ways we encounter experience, that is, when "no boundary yet exists between personal activity and things." (p. 348). Do we yearn for a dream or are we in one?

I return now to you, the reader, whom I left atop the telephone pole, where I have stood, metaphorically, for so long. The literal experience I had occurred about 13 years ago on a ropes course. I remember shouting to those below, saying it wouldn't be so bad if the pole would just stop shaking. The reply that came back was, "no, the pole's not shaking, you are!" And yet, even with that awareness, I could not stop shaking. How do I confront this moment when I feel the pole is shaking me, even though I understand that I am shaking the pole? How do I act in this moment when I know the ground beneath my feet has been my mind, and when I know that everything I think is only thinking? And yet, I can't stop thinking.

This is the background out of which my relation to the moments developed. It was like being presented with a koan. Koans are part of the history of Zen Buddhism, they are devised by Zen masters "to stop their students' word-drunkenness and mind wandering," that is, they present a question or a dilemma that cannot be understood by the rational mind, by thinking (Reps and Senzaki, 1957, p. 111). A well-known koan is the question, what is the sound of one hand clapping? Moments, like koans, present a paradox.

Stern (2004) discusses this paradox in terms used by the ancient Greeks, that of chronos and kairos. Chronos refers to that aspect of moments that occur in time, that is, they have a duration, they exist in the time it takes for something to happen, a passage of time forward into the future. I used this idea in requesting people to share their moments,

DOI: 10.1057/9781137300577

"experiences lasting up to about 10 seconds." Moments, however, also have the subjective experience of nowness, of kairos, "a moment in which events come together and meet, and the meeting comes into awareness as a coherent aggregate" (Stern, p. 367). This aspect of moments was also reflected in the instructions to the subjects, to describe a snapshot of experience. Chronos is linked with linear time, and therefore with story, with narrative. When I tell someone about a moment, the act of communicating requires a translation of experience into a sequence of happenings. This sequencing orients us in time and space and gives meaning to experiences, particularly those events that deviate from expectations. In the sharing, moments are placed within surrounding circumstances, whether within a more limited event (Pillemer, 1998) or a larger life story (McAdams, 1993). From the view of chronos, a single moment can be further dissected, creating a micro-narrative within a moment of experience, whereby the happenings in the moment are also sequenced in a time frame of seconds (Stern, 2004).

Kairos, on the other hand, need not be linked with linear time. A moment, as subjectively experienced, is a gestalt, something whole in itself. Thus, a moment has a different sort of coherence than narrative coherence. Narrative coherence is constructed and reconstructed, marked by an ordering and organizing of experience. Experiences are sequenced causally and temporally into recognizable plots, bringing meaning or interpretation to what happened. Often, such experiences teach us about cause, about human intention, about what we would like to approach or avoid in the future. It is this translation, interpretation or organization of experience that is subject to more or less degree of influence by the discourses of the social/cultural/historical milieu in which we live. Thus, narrative coherence is constructed.

Moments, however, have an inherent coherence. They are experienced as a gestalt or "whole happening" consisting of "the phenomenal content of a bounded stretch of awareness or consciousness" (Stern, 2004). They emerge spontaneously, coming into being, arising naturally in the living of life. They are formed implicitly, outside of awareness, but enter into our consciousness. As such, moments are not the verbal account of experience; they are the raw material for such accounts. Stern (2004) has argued that moments are the basic psychological units of lived experience that make up our larger narratives. When we have a moment, its internal coherence is the mark of its phenomenological status as a moment. Its occurrence is apodictic, we need no further proof of the

DOI: 10.1057/9781137300577

experience. In this light, narrative coherence appears as an overlay onto an inherent coherence that exists in the moment as moment. During the experiencing, moments have a timeless quality. They occur, we are within them, and yet, it is only after they are over that they become bound within the time and space of the occurrence, bound within the past, within a narrative.

Moments, viewed from the perspective of kairos may partake more of our right brain than our storytelling left brain. Jill Bolte Taylor, a brain scientist who suffered a stroke affecting the left hemisphere described how the loss of her left brain functioning profoundly altered her experience of her self and the world (Taylor, 2009). There was an absence of the normal physical boundedness of her body; she perceived herself more like a fluid than a solid, atoms and molecules vibrating in a boundless sea of dynamic activity, an "eternal flow." (Taylor, 2009, p. 71) Without her language center telling her who she was with all her likes and dislikes, she was no longer bound to any self-induced limitations, including all in her life that brought her stress or raised hostility. Gone too was her inner clock that broke the moments of her experience into consecutive instances. Experience was no longer divided into past, present, and future; rather, every moment existed in perfect isolation, perceiving only what was right here, right now. Loss, both physical and emotional, was impossible for her to perceive because she did not experience separation or individuality. She states, "a peace pervaded my entire being and I felt calm" (p. 73).

Without such an injury, our right and left brains contribute to the perception of experience, linked together through the corpus collosum. Taylor's experience, however, highlights the experiential emphasis we place on the narrative functioning of the left-brain and how this narrative functioning is intimately related to the experience of the self. The left brain, with its storytelling, meaning-making function emerges developmentally in the second year of life and, with maturation and the guidance and promptings of caring adults, the stories we tell grow in complexity and detail into adolescence and adulthood (McAdams, 1993; Bruner, 1986). In accord with Taylor's experience, these personal narratives have been strongly tied with the sense of self and the construction of identity (McAdams, 1993; Giddens, 1991). Indeed, in the last few decades, narrative has taken a central role in psychology, the social sciences, and the humanities and is viewed as one of the principal ways humans organize experience in the world. Our narratives orient us in time and

DOI: 10.1057/9781137300577

space, providing coherence and continuity by sequencing events in our lives within recognizable patterns or plots (Bruner, 1986; Sarbin, 1986). Narratives also give meaning to experiences, particularly those events that deviate from expectations (Bruner, 1986). Taylor notes that her left brain was particularly gifted at identifying patterns. She also experienced how, based on minimal information, her storyteller would fill in the gaps in her knowledge, in essence, making up stories and then redundantly replaying loops of these thought patterns.

This storytelling function can be seen, perhaps most starkly, in another neurological condition, Korsakov's syndrome, described by Oliver Sacks (1970/1987). In someone with that condition, there is no memory of the past, and no memory of self or others. But instead of an experience of peace and eternal flow, as experienced by Taylor, there is a frenzied narrative making, making meaning to fill in the gaps, confabulating facts as to what one is seeing, who one is seeing, and what is going on (Sacks, 1970/1987). When visiting Mr. Thompson, a patient with Korsakov's, Sacks says he is variously misidentified and pseudo-identified "as a dozen different people in the course of five minutes. Mr. Thompson would whirl, fluently, from one guess, one hypothesis, one belief, to the next, without any appearance of uncertainty at any point – he never knew who I was, or what and where *he* was, an ex-grocer, with severe Korsakov's, in a neurological institution." In his desperate need to make meaning, Mr.Thompson continually creates a world and a self to replace that which is being continually forgotten moment to moment. From this, Sacks states, "narrative *is* us, our identities." To be deprived of our inner narrative is to be driven, like Mr Thompson, to a "narrational frenzy," ceaselessly telling tales, confabulating, in a mania of mythmaking (p. 111).

Without an inner narrative, we are either, as Taylor experienced, peaceful, one with the eternal flow, in each timeless moment, with no separation of time or form, or we are frenzied narrative makers, clutching to the meaning we ourselves create in each moment, filling in gaps in our knowledge without awareness. What is the difference? I am not a neuroscientist, but it seems that in Taylor's case, she still has an intact memory for the past, she just doesn't hold onto it or make a story out of it. In Mr. Thompson's case, his memory is gone and all that is left is the storytelling function, making meaning as best it can from what little experiential data he has in each moment.

These are limit cases and not representative of non-injured functioning, but they point to a tension or tensions we hold as human beings.

DOI: 10.1057/9781137300577

The tension between the left and right brains, between holding on and letting go, between fear and peace, frenzy and stillness, time and eternity, and self and no self. As they are fundamental to our experience as human beings, these tensions will manifest in a multitude of idiosyncratic circumstances that make up the everyday. They are more or less in awareness, felt more or less intensely, and undoubtedly associated with emotion.

Experiences occur, they impress themselves upon us, we are impacted, and we feel it. If it is a new experience, we will want to make sense of what happened, to make meaning, to integrate the experience and make choices so that the hurt, pain, anger, loss, grief, doesn't happen again or so the joy and happiness is maintained or likely to repeat. How do we choose one thing or another? What will the consequences of each choice be? Can I predict an outcome? At issue is epistemology, how do I know, and ethics, how do I choose.

Charles Sanders Peirce (1955), an American philosopher and mathematician proposed in 1877 that we look pragmatically for some ground that is secure enough to allow one to move from doubt to action. He suggested four ways we seek such ground. The least successful in his view was the method of tenacity, that is, holding on to one's belief even in the face of contrary evidence or others' opinions. Next is the method of authority; this silences disagreement, but often brutally. This method is longer lasting than the first, but cannot suppress doubts indefinitely. Then, there is the method of congruity, allegiance to a current fashionable paradigm; this is more intellectual and respectable, promoting conformity less violently. Peirce posits the most successful method is the last, the scientific method, because it is fallible and open to revision. He states however that reason is most appropriate for theoretical research and may not be best suited for practical matters.

The doubt expressed by Peirce with the search for general laws as the answer for the practical questions of life was the reason why so many have turned to narrative. Within psychology, Sarbin (1986) posited narrative as a viable alternative to the positivist paradigm, which had created a malaise, a crisis of disillusionment in the field. Trying to discern the vicissitudes of social behavior in the laboratory produced little in generalizable results. He pointed instead to the "universality of the story as a guide to living." Sarbin (1986) states, "Long before there was a science of psychology, men and women created and told stories about the efforts of human beings to make sense of their problematic worlds" (p. vii).

DOI: 10.1057/9781137300577

But, why is there such an effort to make sense of our worlds, to construct stories, and to tell and retell them? First, I should be clear that I am using the term story or narrative quite broadly to include theory as well as cultural discourses and personal stories. The scientist as storyteller is not a new idea (Gergen and Gergen, 1986). We hold onto theory just as we can our stories of ourselves, letting them go only gradually with doubt, dissension, and feelings of loss. If one compares the mourning process that John Bowlby describes after the loss of an attachment figure to Thomas Kuhn's description of how scientists move from one paradigm to another, there are marked similarities (Bowlby, 1980; Kuhn, 1962). Given that how we have made sense of our worlds has changed, sometimes dramatically, over the course of time, it is a valid question to ask, why do we rely so much on our stories, our theories? Psychologically they provide a sense of coherence and continuity, but what price do we pay for the feelings of familiarity and order? Social psychology reveals the pervasive existence of biases and attributions of different varieties, wherein we see that which we already believe, and gestalt perception shows us we can't help but see order even when what is in front of us is incomplete. Our personal stories, just as cultural discourses, reveal the structures, images, feelings, ideals, intentions that govern our lives. Our stories focus our attention on these habits and the consequences thereof. Taken together, the experiences of Jill Bolte Taylor and Mr. Thompson, as well as the field of narrative identity, point to our stories as what provides a sense of self; as Oliver Sacks stated, we are our narratives. But, why do we hold onto them so tightly? What would we be without our stories? Would we be annihilated as selves? Is the dichotomy of self versus no-self embedded within many of the tensions we hold, a kind of keystone tension? What would it mean to not have a self...would we experience the peace of the eternal, just as Taylor did? If so, why not trade a self for that? Is it that which is associated with the annihilation of the self that is on the table? Instead of my seeing, my hearing, my touching, my tasting, my smelling, my feeling, there would only be seeing, hearing, touching, tasting, smelling, and feeling.

Perhaps this is too simplistic a way of looking at the issue. Questions regarding the origins, function, and essence of the self have proven it to be an elusive construct. Is the self a unitary entity (Aristotle, 1965); is it a duality of subject and object (James, 1890/1963)? Is the self a cognitive construct (Mead, 1934)? Is it actively constructed by the infant through interaction with others? (e.g. Mead, 1934; Erikson, 1963; Kelly

DOI: 10.1057/9781137300577

1955; Merleau-Ponty, 1964; Vygotsky, 1962; Mahler, 1963, 1967; Kernberg, 1976; Kohut, 1971, 1977). Is it linguistic, as the field of narrative identity suggests (e.g. Bruner, 1986)? Or, is it biological (Damasio 1999)?

There is a deep connection between story and self, but Damasio (1999) proposes, based on neurobiology and neuropsychology, that the autobiographical self is not the root of our sense of self. The autobiographical self is the self that is extended in time. The present is sensed, but it is "flanked" on the one side by the past and on the other by the anticipated future. I am reminded of what Ricouer said of narrative identity, that it is the answer to the question of time. He did not say it was the answer to the question of self. Damasio (1999) takes on this question.

Our autobiographical selves require memory and reason, but language is not essential. Damasio (1999) believes bonobo chimpanzees have an autobiographical self and speculates some dogs do as well. In humans, the extended self is certainly more elaborated, buttressed by our substantial endowments of memory capacity and reasoning ability, together with the gift of language. But, our narrative self is dependent upon a transient, biologically-based, non-linguistic core self. The core self exists solely in the here and now, with no before and no after, and is not dependent on long-term memory, working memory, reasoning, or language. Rather, it is based on the moment-to-moment monitoring and mapping of the states of our bodies as they interact with and are changed by objects in the environment.

The change in these states that occur in relationship creates *a* feeling of what happens, that then becomes *my* feeling. It is within the "highly constrained ebb and flow of internal organism states," ranging from pleasure to pain, wherein the foundation of the sense of self lies (Damasio, p. 30). It is our body states that ground us. In comparison to the myriad changes we perceive as we move through our daily environments, the changes in our body states are relatively highly constrained. This asymmetry, according to Damasio (1999), is what provides a sense of relative stability within our organism in comparison to the external world and supports the continuity of reference we sense as self. Thus the bioregulatory mechanisms occurring at the cellular level to maintain life and homeostasis are the basis for feeling *a* feeling as *my* feeling (Damasio, 1999).

The connection between the body, feelings, and the self, proposed by Damasio (1999), has significant implications for understanding the role that stories and moments play in our lives. It means that to give up our stories would not mean we give up self, quite the opposite, that we would

DOI: 10.1057/9781137300577

be living ever more presently in the ground of self. Instead, by living within a storied meaning, in whatever form it takes, theory, discourse, culture, personality, extended self, we are abdicating to some degree a present response to the situation that is now happening, relegating that decision to a past circumstance, a past outcome, to our conditioning.

If our stories provide a sense of order, coherence, and meaning to our lives, then the fear may arise that without our stories we would be plunged existentially into an ocean of meaninglessness. But is this just another story we tell ourselves? It is the surrender to the annihilation of the extended self that our stories keep at bay, and that to which moments disrupt and intrude upon, providing the complicating action (Labov and Waletzky, 1967) or trouble (Burke, 1952) that narrative entails. But, do we really need these stories, these ways to make sense of our experience? Could we instead have our experience within a momentary assignment of meaning, at the edge of a precipice, responding into the unknown now. I am suggesting that the price we pay for the order and coherence we construct for our lives is the very real relinquishment of responsibility for choosing anew in this moment and the next and the next ... until the story ends.

Further, if culture is a reflection of self, that "man is an animal suspended in webs of significance he himself has spun" (Geertz, 1973, p. 5), then we are also discussing the disruptions, the alterations, and the annihilation of cultures. Thus, there are personal and political reasons to promote the debate of discourse. A discourse comes from the Latin, discursus, meaning "a running to and fro" (RHDEL, 1966, p. 410). It doesn't matter the discourse, what matters is the running.

And yet, we do run, we make stories, we have a left brain. The narrative turn has taken us from reliance on general laws and placed us within the interpretive context of our lives. This was a needed step. But, to the extent we are living within the frame of our stories, we are, each of us, blind, and so too our respective cultures. What the narrative turn has done is to shift our focus from semantic memory to episodic memory. The criticism of reliance on semantic memory is that it decontexts experience. Reliance on episodic memory places experience within a context, but the identificatory process of narrating, extends and rigidifies context. It is as if we are wearing a set of temporal blinders that force the periphery, focusing us on past meanings and anticipations of the future, at the expense of a more full experiencing of now. I am arguing that with the focus on narrative as a primary way we experience ourselves, others

DOI: 10.1057/9781137300577

and the world, the pendulum is swinging too far away from what is happening right now.

This is not a fault of narrative. Narrative is how we make sense of the world. We cannot help but to do this; we have a left brain narrative function. Our narratives foreground our sense of who we are, what we believe in, and how the world is. Our stories represent a line, an interpretation, a translation, a meaning culled from lived experience. They tell us what happened and what we did when the unexpected came upon us, when the trouble occurred. When such experiences are traumatic, particularly if they occur early on in our lives, they deeply condition us to respond in old ways to new circumstances, thus repeating the past over again, the original intention now out of awareness. Trauma need not be acute for this to occur. The attachment, developmental, and psychoanalytic literatures discuss the long lasting impact of cumulative traumas, such as missed attunements between child and caregiver, which over time cause non-optimal adaptations in socio-emotional functioning. Many may not interpret these experiences as trauma or even remember that they occurred. Adults with a particular type of insecure attachment, labeled dismissing, have learned to deactivate their wants and needs to the point that the reported positive nature of the relationship to their parent cannot be supported with illustrative examples or, if produced, remembered episodes reflect contradictory experiences, such as neglect or rejection (Main, 2000). This is just one example of the ways in which we can be limited by the familiar structures, the stories, of our lives.

What our moments are telling us is to listen to our selves without all the stories...and yet...this simple thing can be very difficult. I do not believe it is difficult because we have to annihilate or surrender self, although I think that is the fear. It is difficult because we would need to slowly, patiently, and at times, painfully, look at our sense of self, our autobiographical self, become aware of our stories and see how we reenact them both internally and with others. This is the opportunity and responsibility in each moment, first to see our stories and then to choose whether to continue to hold them or let them go. This is not a singular choice either. It is a moment-to-moment response. That is the hold our stories have, the ever working of our left brains, to tell us that if we find order and coherence that we can live there, at least for awhile, at least until the unexpected happens, loss, trauma, death, at least for now.

But, life happens, not in stories, but in moments. The impact of moments certainly can be influential. They affect our thinking, feeling,

DOI: 10.1057/9781137300577

and behavior, our view of self, our sense of the future. There are moments we want more of, moments to avoid, moments that affirm, and moments that tell us how we would like to be. Moments can change or confirm our stories. Certainly too, there is a need to plan for the future, that is, to make predictions, or to direct our actions (Pillemer, 2003), but it appears that when moments occur, they underscore, not a storyline, but instead, what we do within uncertainty when life is happening, when we are not thinking "about," but instead being "in" or "with" ourselves, others, or the world. The way we organize experience may be storied, the way we construct our self/identity may involve the telling of story to ourselves or others, but, the moments are suggesting, telling us that experience is momentary.

Moments come to us; they simply are, without so much construction or reconstruction. We cannot make moments happen. We only know we have them. Perhaps they hold something of a common language, a way to communicate, even atop that telephone pole, one to another, regardless of how skilled we are at telling our stories or making theory. Moments speak what is, not in some abstract sense, but in their immediate particularity. The moment simply is. It impacts us because, I am suggesting, moments are connected to our core selves more so than our autobiographical selves. A moment can start a story, end a story, or be the point of telling a story. One moment can open us more to the next moment or limit us to avoid what might happen again. But, more importantly, moments are telling us how to live, to notice, amidst all the story telling, the feeling of what is happening in the moment. All the questions about what to do, how to live, how to respond, even who one is, are answered within the grounding of a moment, if only we stop our stories long enough to feel and listen.

What do I do in this moment? No matter what is here right now, I choose my relationship, my attitude, toward it, but only for now. I take one step and that is all I can ever do. I make a choice, and it has consequences, but I do not have to construct a theory, a story, or a self. Whatever we do in daily life, we do, in just this moment. We can't help but assign meaning, our left brain, narrating function, does that, but we can choose whether to hold onto any particular meaning past the point of its momentary assignment. Could it be that within all the complexities of life, with all the idiosyncratic factors at play in any given moment, that being in the moment, to the best of our ability, is all there ever really is, and the rest is just us shaking the pole?

DOI: 10.1057/9781137300577

Part II
Moments

Abstract: *This section consists of three chapters. Each chapter includes two to four individual case studies drawn from the empirical data collected in the Moments project. The case studies are categorized around three main themes that emerged from the collected moments, Relationships, Change, and Death. In a unique moment to moment format, the author responds to each selected moment using interpretive methods usually limited to literary texts. The source of the interpretation ranges across the social and physical sciences and humanities, including the work of Paul Ricouer, John Bowlby, Martin Buber, Brian Massumi, Roland Barthes, and Luce Irigary.*

Forrest, Kelly. *Moments, Attachment and Formations of Selfhood: Dancing with Now.* Basingstoke: Palgrave Macmillan, 2013. DOI: 10.1057/9781137300577.

1
Relationships

Abstract: *The moments in this chapter are the* Wonderful sad monkey, Just trying to reconcile, Black rocking chair, *and* New York cheesecake. *The moments occur in differing kinds of relationships, between a human and a monkey, a boy and his parents, a mother and daughter, and amongst a family. The interpretive analysis addresses themes including freedom and imprisonment, activity and stillness, unity and division, seeming and being, language, narrative, time, eternity, and love.*

DOI: 10.1057/9781137300577

Wonderful sad monkey

> I shared a moment with a monkey. It was a very sad monkey. He did not look like a happy zoo goer. But, we just stared at each other through these bars, or maybe it was a window, for a really long time. It was really interesting. He looked like he was sort of communicating but just through his eyes. And we just stared at each other and I wanted to hug that monkey.

How does one communicate through the bars of imprisonment? Are the bars always visible in such a circumstance? Here, there is a question about what stood between. Was it bars or a window? A window, more than bars, has the potential to be opened, by latch or break. Bars, or more accurately, bars in their juxtaposition with the spaces between are already open, but both, window or bars, tease the gaze toward a horizon that is held unchangingly distant.

We learn the monkey is "very sad." How was he communicating this? How was he holding his body? How close was he to the bars? Were his fingers grasped around them or were his arms down at his sides? Was the body part of the communication? There is no mention of this; no sense of the body other than the eyes. They stared at each other. The staring conveys a stillness, not the pacing or other habituated motion one can see in caged beings. Is he still within or has the energy for movement been placed within the eyes, as they are what may roam? How is the sadness conveyed through the eyes? Is the sadness tinged with hope, with lost hope? He was "very sad," yet he was looking through his eyes. So there had to be some trust in relatedness, or else the energy would retreat, going behind the eyes to some inward place, there and not there, as humans can when they dissociate within or by routine, when there is nowhere else to be, no place that can hold existence.

The activity is shared, "we just stared at each other." These two beings, however, do not share a past together. They are meeting for the first time, an accidental encounter at a zoo. There is an asymmetry between the human and the monkey. How is communication possible? They "speak" different languages; there are differences in history and experience, yet they seem to "sort of" communicate, a feeling is perceived and an intention is evoked. The feeling is sadness. Doubt plays a role, conveyed within the "sort of." Is there a real communication going on? Is the perception accurate? It doesn't seem that it would be difficult to convey sadness to another non-verbally, even if only through the eyes. Sadness

DOI: 10.1057/9781137300577

is about loss and desire, a loss of what was or would have been, and the desire that what is be instead what was or would have been. It is an ache for the familiar, whether real or illusory, a longing conveyed with a look, a look to that which is no longer, to that which may never be. There may be doubt about the communication, but doubt is also part of sadness, the doubt of living with this lack.

It is easy to imagine, if not empathically feel, that a being behind bars would be sad. On the one hand, we can imagine, without more context, there is food, shelter, freedom of movement within a certain bound, and objects for distractive absorption. Perhaps there is work, of a sort, fashioning available items for use, and play, and, at times, companionship. Some enclosures are larger than others, some more thoughtfully constructed, some less so. Yet, life must be adapted to constraints. What naturally arises must be selectively attenuated to those bits that are adaptive to the context. These then become the field of activity, developed and extended, coping as best one can.

Seeing a moment of this, there arose a desire to hug. The desire arose even though, in the circumstances, the hug cannot be completed. There are bars or a window that preclude the hug. Does the desire contain an implicit intention of release? The monkey will stay behind the bars, but if one were to really hug him, the bars would have to be removed. Who is it the desire releases? In the desire to hug there is a desire to draw closer, even if physical touch is hampered. There is also the image of the happy zoo goer, one who enjoys the spectacle of captivity. Is the desire to hug meant to veil this image in a philanthropic intention, a response to an inner dissonance? There is an occluded image as well, that the monkey could be a happy zoo goer. The monkey's sadness does not preclude the implicit release contained within this image. The monkey needs no release, for he, like those who pass by, is a zoo goer, whether happy or sad.

The desire to hug is the second expression of the personal impact of the encounter, the first is "It was really interesting." Here, there is both engagement and distance. Does the desire to hug involve both as well, engaging the distance through an intention to comfort? What comfort is there to one who is captive? Would an offer of escape be the only comfort, outweighing all other? In this circumstance, is such an offer viable? Within the cage, would the polarity to escape arise as well, wanting, needing to hold on to something, anything, with the same energy as the desire to flee? What things are held onto in psychological reactance to prohibitions on living? Can sadness be such a thing? Can happiness?

DOI: 10.1057/9781137300577

What is the monkey experiencing? Jane Goodall, in a recent interview on the 50th anniversary of her fieldwork, said she often wondered how chimpanzees think and perceive the world (December 2011). She said if she could be within their consciousness for a few minutes she would learn more than all her observations combined. Given the extent of her work, this is a significant statement. She spent countless hours in Gombe, Tanzania, observing the social structure and behavior of chimpanzees, and yet, how they experience the world remains elusive.

Could the monkey be viewing the people on the other side of the bars, just as we view him? What is the difference? Humans and primates share 99 per cent of their genomes. The remaining 1 per cent represents differences in 13 places in the DNA sequence, primarily having to do with the opposable thumb. The more salient difference is brain size. This difference has to do with the timing of gene expression, rather than changes in the underlying genes. With the increase in brain size and the power and precision of the grip, humans can speak, write, play music, do mathematics, and throw a baseball. The similarities seem to pale in comparison to the differences, which assist in answering the evolutionary question, what makes humans human. The question of the experience of the other is all too easily distracted, veiled within an inquiry of difference or abstracted to the philosophical. Can we ever know what it is like to be another (Nagel, 1974)?

Aside from genetics and evolution, there is another major difference between the human and the monkey: those visiting a zoo are free to come and go, while the monkey has no such liberty. Humans tend to correlate unfettered movement with freedom. But, there are occasions when humans perceive they are moving when standing still and conversely, that they are standing still when moving. One example is induced motion. The classic illustration is when one is sitting in a stopped train looking out the window and the train on the next rail begins to move. One feels as if the stopped train were moving. One way to counter this illusion is to look for other objects in the field of view that you already know are still and check your position relative to these. This can be tricky, however, if you don't already know what is moving and what is still. The scientific revolution can be said to have begun based on just such a difficulty when Copernicus, contrary to Ptolemy's geocentric model, proposed the earth revolved around a stationary sun. The other way to know which train is moving is to sense motion with your body. This may work on a train, but it still seems to me that I am standing still even though I know I'm moving around the sun. There are other ways humans see motion where

DOI: 10.1057/9781137300577

there is none. One is the apparent motion of scrolling ads on neon signs. The motion is apparent because it is based on flashing a stimulus briefly in one location and then another. Then there is the stroboscopic motion of film involving the rapid presentation of a series of static frames. The point is that humans are easily confused about motion and stillness. Could we be equally confused about freedom and constraint?

Augustine in Book 11 of his *Confessions* meditates on time and eternity (Ricouer, 1990a). Within human experience, things arise, are, and pass away. The experiential world is one of change, of transiency. In contrast to time, eternity is "something that exists that was not created" (p. 23) and is "for ever still" (p. 25). For Augustine, the experience of time as past, present, and future is a function of the activity of mind, of memory, attention, and expectation. This represents the first time that temporal experience is dissociated from cosmological movement. Up to that point, time had been inextricably bound to the motion of the stars.

Augustine laments the activity of mind because it separates him from the experience of eternity.

> But if only their minds could be seized and held steady, they would be still for awhile and, for that short moment, they would glimpse the splendor of eternity which is forever still. They would contrast it with time, which is never still, and see that it is not comparable. (p. 29)

What is perceived in the stillness of eternity? Would eyes no longer be my eyes, but just eyes? With ownership and preferences removed, what would eyes see? Could we see the monkey from such a space; could we see ourselves, much like Copernicus did with the earth? What is it that places bars between beings? Is it sadness? Is it happiness? Is it doubt, doubt that we could hear, that we could listen, that we could see, that there would be anyone there to communicate with? Maybe there isn't much of a difference between coming and going through the world, or being still in a world that comes and goes. Yet, Augustine laments and the monkey is very sad.

I: Has this moment influenced your thinking, feeling, or behavior in any way?

S: No.

I: Has this moment influenced how you think about yourself?

S: No.

I: Do you think this moment will influence you in the future?

S: I think it could. I think more than anything it was just a special moment that only existed in that one place and time. I doubt – I mean, I don't

DOI: 10.1057/9781137300577

really have a lot of contact with animals, so I don't really think – I don't know. It was really, it was interesting that little shared moment with the monkey. But, yeah, no, I think it was a special moment that just gets to live there.

I: Have you shared this moment with others before?

S: I think maybe. In part of my descriptions of what I had been doing abroad and the particular visit, but I don't think that I shared it as though it was like really special to me. It was just like there was this wonderful sad monkey, you know.

Just trying to reconcile

> [I]t was just me sitting down with my mom and my dad at my – this is my later dad; my now dad, he isn't my biological father – and it was me sitting down with them on the couch and I was just trying to reconcile. I was maybe, was maybe like 14 I would say. And I was just trying to reconcile their marriage because I felt like they weren't talking to each other and I was trying to get them to talk to each other. And I – all that it is, is, it's just a very brief image; there's no words. And it's just, it's me feeling really compressed, like I'm just being squeezed, you know. I feel very tight. I feel very tense.

How do we reconcile that which is not in communication, between opposing camps? In logic this position is excluded. It is a law, the law of excluded middle. There is a polarity established between truth and falsity, a line is drawn through consciousness at the start of reason, at least for deductive reason, that process which, unlike induction or analogy, guarantees a conclusion. Experience upon experience cannot make such a guarantee. How can a 14-year-old reconcile an opposition that reason, from the start, requires? The feeling is of being compressed. The word is mechanical, which conjures up compression between opposing forces. But, the source of the compression is eliminated, it is coming from within, "it's me feeling really compressed." The source is hidden, transferred to an effect. They are not talking to each other; yet, there is a shrinking of space for another's existence. When there is a break in unity, what happens is not that a space opens up, as one might think, but rather that a space that was open is felt to be closing, closing in. I am reminded of those images that can be viewed in two ways, the young woman/old woman, or the vase and two faces in profile. Each view alternately occludes the other; there is no middle space. In the actual space of a break, this lack of middle is felt as a compression. Is this true of all

DOI: 10.1057/9781137300577

oppositions, a distance that is apparent only, one that is counterbalanced by a felt compression elsewhere, but precisely because it is felt elsewhere, it is not registered as part of the process? There is the feeling of "being squeezed." Here the source has at least implicitly arrived. To be squeezed comes from outside one's self. But, that is as far as it goes. The description moves back to feeling tight and tense, words carrying no link to source, to responsibility.

In not talking, there need not be a lack of communication. That was seen earlier in the Wonderful sad monkey. There can be communication with no words, at least, "sort of." There, on the couch, there were "no words." If there were no words, was there a communication through seeing, as with the monkey? Perhaps, there was. They were sitting on a couch. We do not know the direction they were facing. In imagination, the 14-year-old sits in the middle, one parent on each side, but each parent's gaze does not look to another. Rather, each looks straight ahead or with eyes averted from the others; the 14-year-old alternately looking down and hesitatingly toward each parent. So, maybe there was no seeing, just feeling as the image conveys. Yet, the moment implies a lack of awareness on the part of the parents to the child's feelings. Otherwise, it seems, the moment would not have happened. Would it be more faithful to this incomplete picture to characterize this lack as a not hearing or not listening? The parents must be hearing something. There is no indication their faculty of hearing is compromised. The "not talking," however, conveys a separation rather than a non-verbal communication. This points to a not listening, an avoidance of whatever is within what is heard. To what are the parents not listening? Conversely, the avoidance is an activity that requires the deployment of attention, consciously or unconsciously. To what are they attending?

There were three people sitting on a couch. They must be fairly close together in physical proximity, perhaps touching in a place along a thigh, shoulder, or upper arm. They would each be breathing in some rhythm. There would be some physical movement as one rarely holds still for very long. Movements of the head, face, mouth, and eyes are likely to be occurring, as are slight body movements. The feelings of tension, tightness, compression on the part of the 14-year-old would be observable, even if subtly, perhaps a holding of the breath, a holding still of what would rhythmically proceed or normally adjust.

The attention must have been in some way inflexible so as not to respond to what is the, admittedly unreported but imagined, rich non-

DOI: 10.1057/9781137300577

verbal world. That this world is imagined does not make it improbable. The 14-year-old is hearing the not talking. It is one of the two salient features of the moment. Is the inflexibility of attention the source of the distance, the split, manifesting as a felt constriction? Rigidification is the end product of the process of differentiation, such splittings focusing attention ever more narrowly on ever more finely nuanced opposites. All words carry within them a division, a definition bounding that which it is from that which it is not. To where or whom does the resultant compression go from all our words? It would be easy here to transfer the responsibility to language. To what use do we put our talking, our not talking?

The intention is stated, "I was just trying to reconcile." To try is to make an effort, yet its focus is on the attempt, distancing the activity. It wasn't stated, I was reconciling. If one says I am attempting to climb a tree versus I am climbing the tree, there is a difference. In the former, failure is implicit in the attempt, or at least, a doubt whether what one is doing refers to the action. The focus on the attempt must mean there is no sense that any reconciling is actually taking place. The parents are not talking. So, the attention is placed on the intentional effort, on trying to reconcile.

In the initial statement, there is no stated object of the reconciliation. We don't know until two sentences later what was trying to be reconciled, the marriage. The enormity of the task is revealed and hinted at by the intervening sentence. The person trying to reconcile is 14 years old and it is not an argument that is at issue, but the entirety of a marriage. Something that was united is now divided and there is an attempt to bring it together. Here are the features of the human condition, unity and division, with the attempt to reconcile.

It is important that there are no words. It cannot be words in this moment that are keeping them not talking. It must therefore be the relationship to words, words we hold onto, identify with, words that regulate identity, self-esteem, or control, words that organize consciousness, that myopically shut out the transfer of responsibility to another for mediating a split that must, at least in the moment, serve the need of individual coherence.

Black rocking chair

> The next moment that comes to mind is sitting in a rocking chair with my mother. It was in our living room. And I still have the rocking chair. It's a black rocking chair. And we got it at, they used to save, my parents used to

> save these green stamps. I think they were called green stamps. And you put them in a book and you got them from cereal or food or, you know, wherever. And then you took them into the store once you'd collected them and you could get merchandise for them. And I remember my mom rocking me in the chair and thinking so this is what a mother's love is, because my mother, I'm sure she rocked me when I was a baby, but my mother never touched me or was affectionate with me or I never felt loved really, just for me, for my accomplishments or for being a cute little girl. I felt like I was, you know, people gave her kudos for having a good little girl or a cute little girl. I never felt loved. And at that moment, I felt loved and thought why haven't I gotten this before and I wonder if I'll get it again. And just for, the only thing I remember is, I don't remember, I mean, I know what the room looks like, but in that moment, I don't remember the room. I just remember sitting and I was snuggled up against her and had my arm behind her, and all I can see is the black rocking chair. And I don't even see my mother. I can feel my mother. And I guess I don't even see me, but I feel me. But it was just the energy that was there at that moment. And along with that love was also a sense of loss because I don't, that is the only time I can remember feeling that from my mom to this day.

The moment begins with an overview, "sitting in a rocking chair with my mother." Attention is placed first on the rocking chair, where it was, that she still has it, and that it was black. This attentional focus continues with a description of how the rocking chair came to be in the living room. The process took patience and care. Green stamps were collected from cereal or food, pasted individually into books, taken to the store, and redeemed. The rocking chair was not purchased directly; it came to be in the living room as a benefit or gift, coming indirectly as a part of other daily activities. Was the rocking chair intended, something the parents wanted, or accidental, happening to be there when the book of green stamps was full and taken to the store? So far, the moment has been about a piece of furniture. There is a sentence left unfinished, "I felt like I was, you know...." How would that sentence have been finished? Did she feel like a piece of furniture? Was the care taken in obtaining this piece of furniture also taken in regard to her?

This wasn't just any piece of furniture; it was a rocking chair. Rocking chairs bring up images of home, hearth, front porches, pondering, contentment, a soothing or comfort connected with the rhythm of back and forth. As a verb, "rock" has two definitions. The first is the one that readily comes to mind, "to move back and forth, esp., rhythmically." The second escalates the force such that the rhythmic quality results in a

DOI: 10.1057/9781137300577

polar experience: "to shake or sway violently, as from a blow" (Webster's, 1984, p. 603). Both experiences are contained within the next sentence. "I remember my mom rocking me in the chair and thinking so this is what a mother's love is ... but my mother never touched me or was affectionate with me or I never felt loved really, just for me ... ." There is no symmetry or back and forth between the loving and unloving experiences. The weight of experience is on the unloving, as if it were possible to keep rocking back in Esher-esque fashion without needing to rock forward. In the developmental literature, this lack of rhythm would be deemed a lack of attunement, interactive error without being followed by interactive repair (Tronick, 1989). There is always error; that is not a problem. What is needed is a response to the error, one that says, oh yes, I forgot that you are here too.

In this situation, would the incongruity of the love she now felt in the rocking chair be felt simultaneously as a blow? Or is the whole of lived experience to that moment reframed as a blow? In between the experience of love and its absence is the parenthetical statement, "I'm sure she rocked me when I was a baby." The connection and disconnection from love is echoed within the unremembered surety; she must have been loved before, but there is no memory of it. Is there care here for the mother, an attempt to minimize or place in context that she was "never touched?" Does it serve as a partial denial of "never" having felt loved? Both represent a transfer of responsibility to herself for not remembering what had been, must have been.

There is recognition of the positive attention her mother received for her being "good" and "cute." The previous implication, based on an uncompleted verbalization, that she felt like a piece of furniture, gets some validation in the objectified role she played for her mother. Any attention she received was felt in relation to this maternal intention. The deflective intent of the unremembered surety gains validity from the statement made directly now, "I never felt loved." The need of the mother is no longer at issue; the impact in felt experience is simple and clear.

It is at this point in the description that the awareness of time arises within consciousness, the present rupturing into the past and the future. "And at that moment, I felt loved and thought why haven't I gotten this before and I wonder if I'll get it again." In *Time and Narrative*, Ricouer (1990b) describes, at the level of history, the schism that can occur between the past and the future as a crisis that requires a response. In the context of a semantic analysis of time, the past is viewed as the space of

DOI: 10.1057/9781137300577

experience and the future as a horizon of expectation. The space of experience is more than the past structuring present experience. It includes all the "possible traversals" from past to present, a multilayered structure rather than a simple chronology. The horizon of expectation is that toward which the consciousness of a historical age is directed, including hope and fear, wishes, and choices, "every private or public manifestation aimed at the future" (p. 208). From a transcendental view, history arises within the tension between these two meta-historical horizons.

Such a tension, according to Ricouer (1990b), becomes problematic when it turns into a schism. This occurs when the space of experience contracts to a past that is done and unchangeable, or when the horizon of expectation becomes too distant and uncertain such that expectation is unable to fix itself on a determined future where distinct steps toward its realization are discernible. To avoid such a crisis, each horizon must be addressed. For the space of experience, "the most tenacious abstraction ... the abstraction of the past as past" must be challenged (p. 208). We must reopen the past, "revivify[ing] unaccomplished, cut off, slaughtered possibilities" (p. 216). We also have to connect expectations to the present, making steps we can act upon, resisting refuge in a utopian future that has no anchor in acquired experience. These are not easy tasks. In Ricouer's (1990b) view, modernity has failed in this regard. In modernity, there is an acceleration of history that is contracting the space of experience, making the past ever more passed, while the horizon of expectation is withdrawing faster than we can advance toward it.

Here, on the rocking chair, this little girl is placed as history, needing to mediate the tension between past and future, that mediation which modernity has failed to achieve. At least somewhere in her consciousness, the girl does not view the past as done and unchangeable. There is a slight opening in imagination for a different, perhaps a fictive past, one in which love was experienced, even if unremembered. "I'm sure she rocked me when I was a baby" takes on heightened significance in the context of Ricouer's (1990b) analysis of time because it shows the delicate and difficult task of what may otherwise seem so easily logical to a meta-historian, reopening the past to cut off possibilities. Lost in the semantic analysis of time is the concrete reality of a little girl trying to understand why she wasn't loved. Confronted with such a reality, the protective abstractness of the transcendental tension is revealed. Those quasi-agents, nations and states, the level at which the force of history can be discerned, collapses and becomes individual experience. Time

DOI: 10.1057/9781137300577

opens itself as a wound, holding the pain of love and loss. How does history cry the tears of this wounding? It is for this little girl to ride the "crest of the present" and "recast" the loss of love "into something never heard before," something "simpl[e] and profound[]" (p. 239). To this, I ask, what is the response of history?

In the moment, the little girl responds. Her response is different from Ricouer's; narrative is not what confronts the temporal crisis, at least in the moment. Rather, it is the experience of feeling love. The place is not important. "I don't remember the room.... all I remember is the black rocking chair." Sight is not important. "I don't even see my mother... I don't even see me." But, sight is there. "[A]ll I can see is the black rocking chair." Feeling is present. "I can feel my mother... I feel me." But, what is most salient, that which carries the moment is energy. "[I]t was just the energy that was there at that moment." That energy is described as love.

The experiential answer to the temporal rupture is love. But the tension does not hold; there is a schism.

> I: Has this moment influenced your thinking, feeling, or behavior in any way?
>
> S: Yes:
>
> I: How so?
>
> S: My thinking. If I felt loved that one time, why have I not been worthy to have that love? What's wrong with me that I haven't been able to get my mom's love, just her unconditional love, any other time? Why is it only that one moment that I remember? My actions. I make sure every day to kiss my children, to hug my children, to take them by surprise and hold them so they know I just don't love them when they do well in school or when they do what they're supposed to. Even if they are, even if they've done something wrong, after we're done talking about it, I'll hold them and tell them that I love them, every single part of them. Because I want them to know that they are loved. My feelings. Every single day – I wonder – and I'm just thinking of this now – do I think of that moment because every single day, I do make sure to let my children know that I love them. It's not like I specifically think of that moment, just the feeling that goes with it or what I remember. Just every day I feel unlovable or unloved. I know I am. I know my husband loves me. I know my kids love me. It's just I don't know.

There are two splits here, between loving and not feeling loved and between knowing one is loved and not feeling it. These represent, on a psychological level, the schism wherein history emerges on a transcendental level. Here is where meaning and interpretation intervene;

DOI: 10.1057/9781137300577

where something must take the place of the falling into the abyss, or less metaphorically, of feeling the pain and grief of not feeling loved and of wondering if it will ever happen again. Once again, this is more than modernity has been able to do.

Perhaps, the split between the individual and transcendental levels has a role here. Where does one look on a meta-level to heal the pain that is so paradoxically present and elusive that theory is only beginning to address (Massumi, 2002). The simple "It's just I don't know" stands firm on ground, on the same ground, as literary theory, critical theory, history, and philosophy. This is a substantive simplicity; it needs no defense. The acknowledgment of not knowing, in general, opens the door to both the past and the future; it forecloses nothing, even in the present. In the particularity, however, in not knowing one is loved, the love is saddened into sorrow.

I: Out of these moments, which would you say is the most important to you and why?

S: I would say the second moment [Black rocking chair] is the most important to me because I think everybody should feel loved. And that lack of love just as a human being, just as a child, is everybody's right. And it was such a quick moment if you will in my life where I felt loved and attached to my mother. I have now had a second one through a counselor I found at the health and wellness center where for a moment I felt her love. But it was such an important moment for me because I always feel lacking now. I just never feel loved the way you're supposed to feel loved by your mother, which I think is so basic. I spent a lot of years looking for it everywhere and finally just gave up. And I know I'll never get it back. I'll just never have a mother's love.

Sorrow narrows the space of experience such that even the moment of love as experienced in the rocking chair becomes obscured; its presence the beacon of its absence. In comparison, the moment of love with the counselor, like the love of the husband and children, is minimized if not negated. This is not a judgment; it is said in a descriptive sense with an informed and felt compassion. The enormity of the task of reopening the past becomes apparent in a way that refiguring a narrative interpretation of history sweeps aside. The investigations into the experience of marginalized peoples are necessary because of just such sweepings. What is difficult about narrative reframing in history or psychotherapy is that it can shroud the affective reclaimings of being that such reframings actually require. To be open to love that is present, to allow love to hold a place in one's being, to know that one feels love or felt love, at least for a

DOI: 10.1057/9781137300577

moment, is not a narrative endeavor. The answer is "I spent a lot of years looking for it everywhere and finally just gave up."

Here also, there is no refuge in a utopian future unanchored in acquired experience (Ricouer, 1990b); rather, the conditioning from experience acts as an anchor. The horizon is foreclosed; not initially, there was a search, a protest to the lack, the lack that shouldn't be. Attachment to others, particularly a mother figure, a primary caregiver, is woven evolutionarily into our beings, if for nothing else but survival. A child alone is vulnerable as prey. In what Bowlby (1969/1982) has termed the environment of evolutionary adaptedness, we, human beings, along with other mammals, learned to seek proximity to caregivers when under distress and to anticipate response within defined parameters. The lack of responsivity from others is disregulating on a physiological level. When a mother and infant interact with one another, there is a dance of attunement going on. The interactive smile of the mother evokes a grin from the infant, the infant when over-stimulated turns away, the mother reduces the engagement, the infant calms, turns back toward the mother, and the mother is there. The dance requires two attending, responding beings.

Infants are acutely attuned to faces; neonates imitate facial expressions from birth (Meltzoff and Moore, 1977). In a paradigm called the "still face" (Tronick et al., 1978), a mother becomes facially expressionless to whatever signals to engagement the child is sending. When mother, who has heretofore been responsive, assumes a still face, the child initially attempts to engage with its repertoire of other-directed cues, such as looking. When not met with response, the child will disregulate and show signs of physiological and psychological distress. The child will avert his gaze, lose postural control, withdraw, and may cry. The still face paradigm is a time delimited technique and when the mother returns with normal responsivity, the infant regains its regulation.

Research on infant and adult attachment, which includes rigorous longitudinal studies, however, shows how the interactive history of primary relationships can have lasting effects on socio-emotional development. Such histories influence the experience of time, but there is not one temporal dynamic between the space of experience and horizon of expectation and in none is there a refuge in a utopian future. Inconsistency in responsivity across situations results in a blurring of past, present, and future. Consistent non-responsivity results in an idealistic view, but not of the future, the idealism is about a past that is largely unremembered. The pain of neglect buried beneath the need to not need and

DOI: 10.1057/9781137300577

its replacement with strength and self-sufficiency. Interactive histories which include physical or sexual trauma or loss of an important loved one, if unresolved, manifest as temporal breaks in continuity. It is these temporal alterations that narrative is hailed to heal.

How does one through and by narrative "revivify unaccomplished, cut off, slaughtered possibilities?" (Ricouer, 1990b, p. 216). Even within the psychotherapeutic field, therapists don't want to listen to incoherent narratives; they are disorienting (Singer, Baddeley, and Frantsve, 2008; Salvatore et al., 2006). The goal is for clients to be able to reframe, refigure the past, such that what happened and the context of what happened can be stated in words to another, and to one's self. Narrative is, after all, a primary way in which we orient, order, and give meaning to our lives.

Whose lives?

> I just never feel loved the way you're supposed to feel loved by your mother, which I think is so basic. I spent a lot of years looking for it everywhere and finally just gave up. And I know I'll never get it back. I'll just never have a mother's love.

That's clear. And yet, what happens to the pain that has gone underground, into the body, into prelinguistic or non-linguistic forms, just so another's life, the listener's life, maintains its order, its orientation, its meaning?

> I: What was your experience during this interview sharing your moments that matter?
>
> S: Sadness. And as you asked that question, and you might just have to scrap the rest of this, I'm not here. This was, didn't realize how meaningful this would be for me, this whole – so, I'm kind of floating out here. So my experience with this is that I'm just, it was a lot harder on me than I thought it would be to share those experiences, because I think those moments were all very significant, particular the first two (includes the Black rocking chair). And it was a little overwhelming for me to have to feel that unworthiness and that insignificance to the degree that I did during this interview and I think I kind of, I want to say buffer each day, you know. I'm in here but I don't, I think it's always around me, the feelings, that those moments have left on me, but I don't consciously think about them. And I certainly don't go back to them very often. And you asked me how often I go back to them. And even if I do go back to them, not to the degree that I did today. Did that answer your question?

DOI: 10.1057/9781137300577

New York cheesecake

> One moment in particular is one night when we came home late from New York City and we were all sitting down having New York cheesecake. And it was then, right at that moment that I was the happiest because I was with my close family members. And every single time when I have cheesecake, I just, that thought blossoms into my head. It's one of those moments where I feel so entirely happy. It's beautiful, so.

How often are we with others? This was not a typical night, at least there is an implication that it was not. It involved coming home "late" and "from New York City." Is this context given only to orient the listener to time and place or is there a more substantive link between atypicality and being with? There is a "we" involved, "we were all sitting down," and yet there is no reference to the others as individuals. We are not told their names. We don't know how many people are present. Instead the attention is on the nature of the relationship, "close family members." The otherness of the members recedes into a shared commonality.

This saming of otherness is typical in relationships (Irigary, 2008). We carry a space for others within ourselves, but so often this space is already defined, readymade for *any* other, saturated with our own norms, rules, lacks, and voids. More rare do we open to the other as other and for other. Does the characterization of the family members as "close" mean that each is more open to the other as other or less so?

The family members are "having" New York cheesecake. From the middle English, "have" is derived from haven, a place of safety or refuge. It commonly means to possess, own or hold, to be related to in some way, or to partake. Does the use of the word "have" rather than "eating" carry any significance? It has an effect of focusing the moment on something other than food, even though they are having "New York cheesecake." There were other clear options for attention. New York cheesecake is creamy and smooth due to its high butterfat content, made as it is from heavy cream and cream cheese. The flavor of the cake is relatively neutral with hints of sweet and sour. The sweet is from sugar, cream and vanilla; the sour from a hint of lemon that, remarkably, cuts through the heavy buttery character of the cake giving it a brightness. The crust is ultra thin. The topping is completely variable and could include chocolates, berries, fruits, or nuts complemented with some cream fraiche. The texture, taste, smell and visual aspects of the cheesecake are all in imagination, we are not told.

DOI: 10.1057/9781137300577

The focus of the moment, instead, is on a feeling, of being happy. This happiness is not derived from the cheesecake. The cheesecake, with all its sensual qualities, is a medium, a catalyst for being with, perhaps also a symbol of a day had together that is continuing into the lateness of the night. This quality of happy is powerful. It is being "happiest" and arises "every single time when I have cheesecake."

How does one know one is "happiest?" There is always the polarity that is called up. Kelly (1955) knew about this idea. He created a theory of personality, Personal Construct Theory, based on the bipolarity of our categories, that is, for example, that happy is inextricably linked to unhappy, or sad. It is a theory based in constructivism. People develop bipolar categories, constructs, in order to better know and anticipate or predict events and people's behavior. Kelly said that each person creates a construction system for anticipating events that uses constructs that are dichotomous in structure. His view of how meaning is derived from constructs, however, does not comport with classical logic. In logic, a thing is either B or not B. For Kelly, three elements are required to establish identity, two similar and one contrasting. So, to establish being happy versus sad, one would have to be comparing the New York cheesecake moment to another happy one and also to a sad one. What is the comparison to know that one is "happiest?" How many happy moments are needed as comparisons for that? Or, how many sad moments are needed to elevate a happy time to one that is happiest? Can there be more than one happiest memory? It's the comparison part that is interesting. If I am happy during an occurrence of a happening, while it is happening, I surely will have some concurrent indwelling of feeling, and be able to say I am happy. But, the comparison that seems to be required to say, happiest, would have to be a judgment after the fact. Could I realize later that my feeling of happy, in comparison to other more happy times, was actually, not all that happy, but in fact, more toward the sad side of things? Logically, those types of reinterpretations seem possible. What are we really saying when we say something is the happiest, that all the rest of life was less so?

The thought is described in an unusual way; it "blossoms into my head." Blossoms are the flowers of stone fruit trees, including cherry, apple, peach, and plum. They are pink or white and provide pollen for bees. Blossoms are vulnerable to wind; they are easily torn from their trees, often covering the surrounding ground in petals. Here again, the idea that this happiness is fleeting arises, as a blossom that is so easily taken by the wind.

DOI: 10.1057/9781137300577

The idea of blossom also has an unfolding aspect; the thought unfolds "into my head." How does it unfold? There is no indication that the scene plays itself out chronologically. Rather, the thought is connected to a feeling, "I feel so entirely happy." It is the thought and the feeling together that "blossoms," that is "beautiful." The language, in its own way, expresses the beauty and impermanence of such unfoldings, of beauty, happiness, and being with. "It's beautiful, so."

Why the "so?" This is a mild form of passivity in speech, placing a vague word at the end of a sentence. It could be a placeholder, a way to suggest that the speaker wants to say more but for some reason does not.

> I: Is there anything you would like to add to your description of the moment?
>
> S: Well, I especially notice that we were just talking about something irregular, like nobody else would think about talking about this, like a, such as a – it's embarrassing, but we were talking about belching and you know. It was funny how our family was just so, just made that into a conversation. It was the emotion really, that really made the thought come up most of the time, so. Other than that, I think basically the taste, how – the taste of the cheesecake, the moment of happiness and joy where everyone was just themselves. Nobody had like a show or had something to show. It was just relaxing. It was one of the most comfortable places and where I want to be the most, so. I don't know if you want me to add on to that?

Here, the reference to atypicality is explicit, "we were talking about something irregular." This is also the first that we know there was a conversation going on between the family members and not a sharing in the silent spaces of being with and eating. The family was talking about a bodily function, belching. There is hesitation, embarrassment, about the body's release of gas. And, finally, there is mention of the taste of the cheesecake. Yet, once again, the gustatory or bodily aspects that are reported are foregrounded not for themselves but as indicators for something else, that "everyone was just themselves."

The issue raised is about seeming and being. Martin Buber in *On Intersubjectivity and Cultural Creativity* (1992) describes this as the "essential problem of the sphere of the interhuman" (p. 70).

> Let us now imagine two men, whose life is dominated by appearance, sitting and talking together. Call them Peter and Paul. Let us list the different configurations which are involved. First, there is Peter as he wishes to appear

DOI: 10.1057/9781137300577

> to Paul, and Paul as he wishes to appear to Peter. Then there is Peter as he really appears to Paul, that is, Paul's image of Peter, which in general does not in the least coincide with what Peter wishes Paul to see; and similarly there is the reverse situation. Further, there is Peter as he appears to himself, and Paul as he appears to himself. Lastly, there are the bodily Peter and the bodily Paul. Two living beings and six ghostly appearances, which mingle in many ways in the conversation between the two. Where is there room for any genuine interhuman life? (p. 71)

In social psychology, issues of conformity, particularly normative social influence, speak to this phenomenon most directly – how individuals split themselves for public acceptance. The Asch conformity experiments are the classic illustration of this phenomenon. In those studies, subjects are told they are taking part in a vision test. They are presented with three lines of varying lengths, labeled a, b, and c, drawn on a card. The next card has one line drawn that clearly matches the length of one of the lines on the first card. The subject is asked to match the line to that of a, b, or c. This would be simple except that the subject is not alone during this task. There are 5–7 others who are taking part, however, unbeknownst to the subject, these others are confederates in the experiment. The confederates are appropriately placed so they give their answers to the line task prior to the subject. On particular trials, they give the wrong answer, and on some trials, they all pick an unambiguously wrong line, the same wrong line. The situation is this. The subject sees clearly that the line matches line b, but everyone else says c. What does the subject do? In 75 per cent of the cases, subjects go along with the incorrect answer at least once. It's not 100 per cent and even those that go along at least once don't go along all the time. But, this shows that even in benign situations among strangers, even when there is certainty of perceptual judgment, seeming can predominate.

Buber (1992) says "[t]o yield to seeming is man's essential cowardice, to resist it is his essential courage" (p. 72). Yet, there is more than the struggle with seeming and being that keeps two people from genuine dialogue. Each needs to make the other present, "imagining the real," from within ourselves, the other lives in us, accepted, affirmed, confirmed in their being as partner in dialogue (p. 75). For this, Buber too, uses the word "blossoms," "if mutuality stirs, then the interhuman blossoms into genuine dialogue" (p. 75).

> I: Only if you – right now – I'm going to ask you some questions later about the moment, but right now its just as long as you feel comfortable with your description of the moment, that's all I'm looking for.

S: All right. Well, would you like me to describe the area or do you want me to describe the people that were there or?

I: What I'm asking is that, I'm asking if you have a snapshot of experience that you have had, and in that snapshot, not necessarily all the things that surround it, but what's in that snapshot for you.

S: It's, it's kind of – everyone has a face, an alter face. And in that one moment, not only did everyone relax, it was like a moment where nobody was tense, it was, it was no faces had to be shown, nothing like that had to take place. Nobody had to mask themselves in order to appeal to most people. We appealed to each other because we were family and we've known each other for so long that we do not have to hide ourselves from each other. And it's just a point in realization where I thought to myself maybe I should, you know, come back here even more. Maybe I should – this is, moments like these make me want to stay there forever because in that certain place, it brings up so many – I could touch something and I could remember things, like at the kitchen table. That kitchen table's been there for so long. We come back to it every night. I think about the advantages and disadvantages of living at that place or that certain – but, you know, I would live there no matter how messy, how gross, how bad it is in the house. It still, it holds that many memories. And that one memory particularly comes up because it's not normal for us to, you know, come together, have New York cheesecake. I mean, that's only New York City cheesecake and, you know, sit together. It's one of those family traditions that we hardly do any more, so it's – and this is with family that live far away from me. And it's, it's hard to, you know, go back and forth from place to place. And that moment just sticks out like a sore thumb. So I sit around here and if I go to like cheesecake factory, it's never going to be the same, so.

DOI: 10.1057/9781137300577

2
Change

Abstract: *The case studies in this chapter are based on two moments,* Whoosh ... here I am *and* Set for the ... snap. *Both moments address in different ways what occurs when a new world is encountered. In the first, the arrival in a new country is described; in the second, a moment in youth football. The interpretive analysis of the moments explores change and identity, figure and ground, beginnings and endings, control and chance, the known and unknown, fear, chaos, choice, and justice.*

Forrest, Kelly. *Moments, Attachment and Formations of Selfhood: Dancing with Now.* Basingstoke: Palgrave Macmillan, 2013. DOI: 10.1057/9781137300577.

Whoosh ... here I am

> One that really stayed with me is I was 21 years old. I didn't do a junior year abroad as an undergraduate because I couldn't afford to. I worked 40 hours a week and went to school full time, so I had to save my money. I worked my senior year, so I was older. And I went to ________ University [in England] and matriculated through their University. And nobody in my family had done that before, and so I was sort, didn't really know what to expect. And because I wasn't going with a bunch of juniors, I was going on my own, so I flew from California through the night and got off the plane, went through customs and walked through the doors of customs and just was hit with the smell and the sound of a very different place. And I just remember the quality of light was different. I remember thinking it's really dark. So it was dark and smelled differently. I have a very strong sense of smell and. And then they spoke English, but it wasn't English I had heard. And it just, it just hit me how alone I was. I didn't have a place to go. I had to figure out how to get to the hostel, etcetera, etcetera. So in that moment, I just felt this bottom falling out of my known world and something completely unknown, which turned out to be fine, but for the moment, it wasn't exactly panic but a feeling just like whoosh, like here I am.

This moment reminds me of how Roland Barthes describes the way he looks at photographs in *Camera Lucida* (1980). In his glancing through an illustrated magazine, he came upon a photograph that made him pause. It was a photograph taken during the rebellion in Nicaragua. The photograph consisted of "a ruined street, two helmeted soldiers on patrol; behind them, two nuns" (p. 23). Within the pause, he realized that what allowed the photograph its "existence (its 'adventure')" for him, was due to the "co-presence of two discontinuous elements, heterogenous in that they did not belong to the same world" (p. 23). He saw this as a structural rule that could be the source of his attraction to particular photographs. He named the two elements: studium and punctum.

Studium is from Latin: it refers to a spatial element, an "extent," a "field," a kind of "general interest" one takes that can include an emotional response, but one that is mediated by "training," by "the rational intermediary of an ethical or political culture" (p. 26). The feeling is an averaged one, a "kind of general, enthusiastic commitment ... but without special acuity." Through studium, Barthes has a culturally based interest in a wide array of photographs, allowing his participation in the figures, faces, gestures, settings, and actions, whether they are depicted historical scenes or works of testimony. The studium carries meaning at its most

DOI: 10.1057/9781137300577

basic level, that of intention. Thus, studium carries within it the myths, the "alibis" of the photographer, the reasons for the taking of the image, "to inform, to represent, to surprise, to cause to signify, to provoke desire" (p. 28). Barthes explains his relation to studium:

> The *studium* is of the order of *liking*, not of *loving*; it mobilizes a half desire, a demi-volition; it is the same sort of vague, slippery, irresponsible interest one takes in people, the entertainments, the books, the clothes one finds "all right."

The punctum ... is that which breaks the studium. One's consciousness does not seek for, is not invested in, the punctum, as it does and is the studium; rather the punctum "wounds" the field, arising from it, "shoot[ing] out of it like an arrow, and pierces me" (p. 26).

From where does the punctum arise? What is the source of Barthes' "delight or pain" within the field of the socio-cultural familiar? It is not fascination, Barthes says it is "something more like an internal agitation, an excitement, a certain labor too, the pressure of the unspeakable which wants to be spoken." He settles on the word *advenience*, or adventure.

In this moment, there is adventure. It is placed within the studium of Western culture, that "bastardized marriage between individualism and success" (May, 1991, p. 115), the 40-hour-work week while going to school, the having to do it alone, not being able to afford a junior year abroad, saving money, going beyond what family had done before. Expected too is the flying all night, getting off the plane, and even going through customs. And, then there it is, the punctum, even in the language, "and just was *hit* with the smell and sound of a very different place."

The basis of the punctum is the change from what would ordinarily be focused on when describing a new place; the sights are absent. Light makes an appearance, but only generally, as atmosphere, as "quality" of light and dark. Even within this description, seeing is placed in the background. How does one know the quality of light was different? It is not through seeing, but through thinking, "I remember thinking it's really dark." We don't know if this is outside, although that is implicated, with having "walked through the doors of customs." Yet, it could be inside, that part of an airport that is beyond security, beyond customs, but not yet outside the terminal.

Security and customs within terminals, all in one reflecting an aporia within modern and postmodern cultural theory (for a review, see Massumi, 2002). Where is there a place for change, for adventure, within

DOI: 10.1057/9781137300577

the security and customs of our individual and cultural constructions and positionings, the terminal temporalities and topographies within our lives? Time and space are fixed within a socio-cultural version of Newtonian physics: whereof Einstein's relativity? Do we not want to ask for Newton's forgiveness?

With the punctum, are we talking about the other side of trauma, that which only pierces and wounds the field to awaken it to a differencing from the familiar, to that which goes beyond Barthes' "all right," "liking," to that of "loving" or "pain?" But if there is pain, can punctum also alter the field, changing it, as it can in trauma? The phenomenon of resistance within psychotherapy points to trauma's pull toward sustaining itself, for creating a new familiar, a new "all right." Yet, the all right really isn't all right, it is not a matter of indifference, it hurts, there is pain. Is trauma somehow both field and punctum, or does trauma do away with field altogether, nothing is all right anymore, all is punctum? Is this what suffering is? But, what of punctum's delight, joy, and loving? These are part of the adventure, the best parts, punctum's share in trauma, the nature to awaken from the all right, from the indifferent irresponsibility of the field. Field and punctum together. To pass through is to pass through security, to pass through customs, and to be hit with reality, life with punctum; but not derealized in photographs, not in images. Barthes is pointing the way; so too the moment.

There are smells and sounds. And, "they spoke English, but it wasn't like English I had heard." What do we do when language fails? "And it just, it just hit me how alone I was. I didn't have a place to go." What do we do when positioning fails? We go to "figure[ing] out how to get to a hostel, etcetera, etcetera." Take the next step... get to a hostel, a place of lodging for a night for travelers willing to pay less to share more with others. But, it's not just getting to a hostel, there is the "etcetera, etcetera." What comes next, we don't know. Within the "etcetera, etcetera," could be anything. Will it be the "all right" of the field, or the "delight" or "pain" or trauma of the punctum? Ultimately, we can never know what the future holds, even with assiduous planning. So, the future is there as an etcetera, a testament to our assumption of time, of more time.

The feeling is the "bottom falling out of my known world." The ground gives way with the loss of language (meaning) and spatial orientation (direction, place). Just at this point, hind-sight secures the happening through a punctuated parenthetical reference to the temporal field, "it turned out to be just fine." But, in the moment, in the "something completely unknown," there wasn't the chaos that narrative remedies,

DOI: 10.1057/9781137300577

there "wasn't exactly panic" but instead a "feeling just like whoosh ... here I am."

Is that the fear?

> I: And when you shared this moment in the past have you described it as a short moment of experience or have you included it as part of a larger story?
>
> S: It's part of a larger story.
>
> I: Would you share that story here?
>
> S: Sure, yeah. The larger story is how, how silly I felt to think that English would be so simple because the first people I went to ask for directions to – I had an address for a hostel and I couldn't read the signs, I couldn't figure out what bus to get on, so I went up to several people and asked and all of them had east end accents and I couldn't understand a single thing they said to me and so I stood there thinking, oh, my god, I can't even speak this language and then really feeling like, well, there is no translation for this, it's not like my Italian has to get better, like what am I going to do, this is my language. So I usually tell that story of feeling that something was awfully wrong. That was a horrible moment.

Set for the ... snap

> Yeah, cause I used to play on the Y, I was a Y man. And I remember putting my hand down and getting set for the guy to snap the ball and one of the other guys spit on my hand, the other defensive guy, and so I flinched, you know, then I got the flag thrown. I remember that.

Why play on the Y? Why? This little word carries so much on its shoulders. The question assumes explanation, a causality other than chance or fate, something to point to, some reason. If it were only chance, there is no reason to ask about causation; it just happened by accident, reason has nothing to grasp. Ricoeur (1983) describes the process of constructing causality in narrative. In narrative activity, causality is Aristotle's *di' allele,* the "one because of the other" that forms the logical connection of a plot. The course of events themselves, an episodic chronology, one thing after another (*met' allēle),* is insufficient as explanation. Explanation requires an integration of underlying components, such as actions, obstacles, aids, circumstances and results into a "meaningful unity" (Ricoeur, 1983, p. 178).

This quality of "whole" (holos) stems from the imaginative activity of the narrator that breaks the story out of the field of real action and sets

DOI: 10.1057/9781137300577

forth a beginning, a middle, and an end. This emphasizes, not the temporal, but the logical character of the organization. The beginning, middle, and end are no longer features of experience, but "effects" of a constructed ordering which absents chance and conforms to necessity or probability. Coherence is emphasized and chance disallowed. "To make up a plot is already to make the intelligible spring from the accidental, the universal from the singular, the necessary or the probable from the episodic" (p. 41). Probability reaches its lowest point in the accidental. To answer the question why, the imagination enters. Ricoeur (1990a) quotes Max Weber, "In order to penetrate the real causal relationships, we construct unreal ones" (p. 186). The narrator constructs a point of view that is disassociated from the "confused and limited perspectives" of the characters in the story.

Why do we abhor chance so much? The whole scientific endeavor, including the turn to narrative, is about bringing order and meaning to a world of chaos, a world of contingent happenings outside of human control. What is meaning but the possession or capture of events, a connection of biography to time? In the ancient novel, biography and time connected only at two points, the beginning and the end (Bakhtin, 1981). In between, there is a "sharp [extratemporal] hiatus that leaves no *trace* in the life of the heroes or their personalities" (p. 90).

From the inside, adventure-time "is organized from without, technically." There are a series of separate adventures linked together by the logic of "random contingency." Link words such as "suddenly" and "at just this moment" highlight the importance of chance occurrence, being or not being at the right place at the right time. In adventure-time, chance meetings (simultaneity) and non-meetings (ruptures) interrupt the "normal, pragmatic, premeditated course of events" (p.92). "All moments of this infinite adventure-time are controlled by one force – *chance*. Adventuristic 'chance time' is the specific time during which irrational forces intervene in human life" (p. 126).

Yet, in the ancient novel, biography is untouched by the interventions. Ordeals are endured, but they have no impact on individual development; the human is not used up by its ordeals. In this literary chronotope, time and space are fixed such that biography is distanced from chance but aligned with beginnings and endings. I am reminded of a quote from Pascal.

> For after all what is man in nature? A nothing in relation to infinity, all in relation to nothing, a central point between nothing and all and infinitely far from understanding either. The ends of things and their beginnings

DOI: 10.1057/9781137300577

> impregnably concealed from him in an impenetrable secret. He is equally incapable of seeing the nothingness out of which he was drawn and the infinite in which he is engulfed (Kline, 1980, p. 353).

Why do we play sport? Sport places control on the beginnings and endings of time. In sport, we can call time. Sport has been used as a metaphor to "begin[]" to resolve the postmodern dilemma of determination, that is trying to solve the problem of "[w]hich came first... [t]he individual or society?," the problem of change (Massumi, 2002, p. 71, 68). Change cannot come from individuals because they are subject to the structures of language and society into which they are born and to which their experiences are molded. How can society be the source of change when the relation between people, the intersubjective field, is fixed, positioned, indexed within socio-cultural geographies of language and power?

Sport, however, is about the play, about relation. Sport, as illustrative analogy, locates change within a "logic of relation" (Massumi, 2002). The terms of the relation, the players, the field, are not the source(s) of change, but rather, the relation itself. Massumi builds on earlier uses of soccer to explain. The field of play is a "field of potential," potential for modifying the field through movements (events) of player or ball. The field is "minimally organized" as a "polarization" between "two attractors," the goals. The goals set the physical limits of play, polarize the space, and induce play. Players are acting reflexively and relationally, but not reflectively, to the "contingent intermixing of elements" (players, ball, referee, fans); every gesture polarized to score or repel a goal. Reminiscent of psychoanalytic object relations, players are part-objects, eyes, ears, and touch channeling movement to the foot. The ball is a part subject, catalyzing play, the focus of every player, the object of every gesture, the subject of play.

The "event-dimension of potential" is the dimension of the "inter-relating of elements and their belonging to each other." This belonging, not language or reflection, is "unmediated" and "never already constituted." The belonging is an "open-ended belonging," a "coordinated becoming" wherein change is "emergent relation." Formalized sport and its regulation by rule evolve from an "immanent," unformalized, proto-sport field of potential.

Within the formalized game, it is the referee that stops the action, reflects, and curtails deviations from the rules, maintaining the identity of the game for later repetition. Change can come within the rules, but

DOI: 10.1057/9781137300577

only as "style," as "small, but effective ways of skewing the potential movements," "little extras" like "catching the eye of players on the opposite team to make them self-conscious and throw them off their game" (p. 77).

Interrupting the flow of the action, stopping it, is what creates the seeming that the game is being played amongst separate players in relation to each other, with its inherent problem of determination with no source for change. In stopping the action, the referee "isolate[s] a move" and "pins responsibility" for that discrete movement on a "single playing body," thereby creating the apparent isolation of the body from the immanence of the field of potential. Thus, the rules of play and their application interrupt an "immanent relationality" and yet, the rules and their interruption are part of that immanence. Within this relation, change and identity are opposed, "variation is a departure from identity" (from the perspective of the referee), and "identity is a moment (a productive lapse) in the continuation of variation" (p. 79).

Now, the problem of determination is beginning to be resolved, the picture is emerging of a space for change that isn't a space, but a relation, a coordinated becoming, a belonging. There is a field of potential, of relational movement that is only later captured and codified into rules; movements into post hoc events, regulation serving the need for identity of the game and its repetition across time and location.

Here, the game is football. The Y may be an offensive formation or maybe Y is part of an acronym, short for YMCA. The moment is just before the beginning or resumption of play. In imagination, you can see the blockers, each with a hand down along the line of scrimmage, the ground steadying the starting stance, readying for play. There is all the intermixing of elements, the other players, the ball, the noise from fans, the call of the play, movement, if any, in the offensive or defensive backfield, the referee watching the line, looking for movement where only stillness should be, all part of the field of play, all part of time, of continuity, of the ground of change. Yet, for the game's identity, time has not started. The clock is still. The ball has not yet been snapped.

What is happening? In the moment, in imagination, an image or thought emerges into the mind of a single bodied player. We don't know why. We are told he is a "defensive guy," referring to a role he is playing within the game. The game fixes the positions on the field, as pieces in chess, each with possible moves and no others, a job to do within the immanent relationality. He knows the rules of the game, he knows that

DOI: 10.1057/9781137300577

stillness is called for now, in this situation. But, regardless of the reason, he does not want to chance chance within the bounds of the game. He spits and causes another player to flinch.

Why the spit? Is it a rebellion against the game? This does not seem likely to be salient because such a resistance does not draw attention to the game as problematic, but rather exploits the holes within the game to advantage. The referee can't see everywhere. No, it does not appear that resistance to the identity of the game is at issue. Neither, for the same reason, does it seem an innovative "style" that seeks to evolve the game.

So, why the spit? Now, there are two possibilities, that may turn out to be one. The first is that the spit, even though outside the rules of the game, outside the game's identity, is in fact part of the game. The game's identity is a split one, one official and one unofficially official, two different sets of rules. Perhaps, the referee saw and didn't call it. Boys will be boys; just don't flinch. The second is that the spit is about identity, but not the game's identity. In the mind of the defensive guy, the outcome looms, what if loss, what if chance deals the card that is not preferred. The game is fine, the rules are fine, but he says, on some inner level, "I don't want to chance my self to chance." Chance is an enemy, that which can take something that is needed, something that cannot be lost, something of identity.

Time looms as outcome, as future that holds a possibility, one preferred, one not, an after that matters. Time is foregrounded, in particular, future time, and in specificity, identity's relation to future time, an illusion, but a powerful one. Play recedes into the background, abrogated, rendered dysfunctional in relation to chance, a thought is formed, a thought of driving chance, corralling it. The required stillness in the play must be foreshortened within the illusion of future time; the illusion distracts the stillness to violation, to rig the game, to steal chance, to steal time, to hold identity.

The spit is about identity's relation to time. Identity, A = A, is thought of as something that retains its continuity over time. We see that with the game. If the rules just changed, we would no longer be playing football, we'd be playing soccer or basketball or who knows what. But, we are not talking about the identity of the game, at least not directly, what has arisen against the background is the figure of the defensive guy's identity. What identity does he hold of himself that he spit? I'm a spitter, or I'm a cheater, or I get the job done, or I'm a winner, or I'm not a loser?

DOI: 10.1057/9781137300577

Identity is held across time, defended even into the imagined future. That is what identity is, isn't it? Are we not each of us tempted to move ahead in time, to an outcome for identity, to make steps to meet that outcome, sometimes regardless of means, particularly if the means don't really hurt someone, or sometimes even if they do; that's their problem, just learn not to flinch.

The picture is getting clearer. The figure of identity is held, over time, opposed to chance, opposed to change, even as change occurs. Let's stare at this figure for awhile. Just stare at identity, at the defensive guy's identity and hold it, hold it, hold it, don't look away.

In gestalt psychology, we would say we are now fixing a figure, staring at it, forcing deliberate concentration. Prior to this, the figure was forming out of the context of the moment, out of a more spontaneous concentration, that which allows elements of the ground, in this case, the ground of being, to enter into the figure. But not any more because now we are staring, fixing identity, holding it, holding it, worrying about its future, about what can happen, chance is out there, chance could mean the figure would change, but it can't change, we are holding it fixed, identity fixed against change, we will make it happen, no matter what happens.

What is happening? Fatigue, flight, or if you keep staring, as happens with anything you stare at too long, the figure weakens, starts to blur and disappear. Staring is disintegrative of figure, you enter into a hypnotic trance. Identity as trance. Did the defensive guy spit, reacting out of identity's trance?

Wait, wait, what is happening to identity? I see the problem more clearly now, the problem of determination. The figure is now the socio-cultural categorizations, the topographical grid of possible positionings. There is no freedom for identity to change, only a vault from one position to another. The guy is locked within a relational position in a game, he is a defensive guy, polarized by one of two goals, attractors that potentialize all movement, to score or repel, he repelled, he spit. He is not just defensive, he is a guy too, fixed within a socio-cultural category of asymmetrical gender relations. In football, if you are a guy on a team of guys, who are those on the other team? You are locked into these categories, someone has to be the other, he spit. This is why identity is opposed to change, I see, yet, no, now I don't see clearly.

Now the figure is immanent relationality and the moment disappears. The defensive guy is gone, he's now a term, the spit is gone, the flag is

DOI: 10.1057/9781137300577

gone, the flinch is gone, these are "movements" that, once "captured" are "events," and memory is gone. Do terms have memory? All is intermixed, all is relation, the terms are only seemingly external to the relation, all is coordinated becoming.

Where did the moment go? It went into the background, which is necessary to make the figure, immanent relationality, more clear, so that there is a process across the gaps of positionality, for movement, for change, to connect body to culture. The point of contact is the boundary of the (substantial/actual) potential. Where is that? At the boundary of the infraempirical (too small to perceive) and the superempirical (too large to perceive). I could't really get much further than this with Massumi. I know it had something to do with needing to find a "cultural-theoretical vocabulary specific to the body" (p. 66).

What is happening? Well, it appears that the ground (immanent relationality) is now the figure, but by staring at it too long, it became blurry, as can happen when you stare at a figure, and there are times when I think immanent relationality is not a figure, only a very highly charged ground, which leaves one wondering where to look. Can you have a ground with no figure? Let's go back to the football moment. Where did identity go? The identity of the game is conserved, but what about those "terms," here the defensive guy? It, sorry, he too went into the background, as is most of the organism/environment boundary, except what I assume would be Massumi's view, the ball/hand contact boundary, all out of awareness, all ground.

So, is identity opposed to change, or is identity, at the level of the terms, simply irrelevant to change because change occurs at the level of "little extras" within the game structure? Or, is it most clearly said, that identity at the level of the terms is assumed to be fixed because identity is opposed to change because we are holding it fixed? Hence the problem with determination in cultural theory and continuity and discontinuity in narrative identity work. Or does identity not matter, really, because, now that we have movement accounted for, in fact, all of ground is movement, or is that the figure, well, it doesn't matter, since we have movement, we don't need to worry whether identity changes or not, or even whether there are identities.

From a Gestalt perspective, the problem we are encountering is one of a "too-forced figure" or a "too-charged ground" (Perls, Hefferline, and Goodman, 1951, p. 59). Gestalt psychologists have known this and been working with this since the 1950's. We are stuck on a figure or we

DOI: 10.1057/9781137300577

get distracted by the ground. The movement that everyone seems to be looking for is right where no one is looking, an open secret, you might say, but one of which the existential-humanistic phenomenologists are well aware. The movement is a natural attentional one, the movement of allowing a figure to emerge out of a background and then allowing another figure to emerge. There is always a figure/ground gestalt, but what is included within a figure and what is in the ground are not static.

As a figure begins to emerge, ground is everything else that gets progressively removed from the experience. As the figure changes, what is in ground changes as well. There is a natural free flowing dynamic relation between figure and ground. This is the writing style used by Massumi, which I like by the way even if the figures fail to fully cohere, which is consistent with the comparison of his writing to a "black hole" (Massumi, 2002, p. 17). If the figure is clear, unified, and bright, and the ground is empty, it is a strong gestalt. If the figure is not well formed, it is termed a weak gestalt.

This is a natural process, but one that can get interrupted. As earlier mentioned, attending to a figure too fixedly, that is holding it with more deliberate attention, does not allow anything new to emerge spontaneously from interest out of the ground to enter into and change the figure. Or, the ground can be too charged, holding too many points of attraction for interest such that attention is divided and a figure never unifies in clarity. In extreme, this is the experience of chaos.

We live in a world of multitasking, of divided attention, with multiple sources of attractions which easily distract. We also fear chaos. It is no wonder that narrative's ordering of experience and identity's unifying figure are held, even if too fixedly. We would rather be fatigued, in flight, or in trance, than be in chaos. Just do your job, you have a position, you are a term. Your freedom is in your style, those accessories that show your vision of being a term, in your position, of course. So, it's back to finding a place to fix attention, on style, and hold it there, style as identity. His style is to spit.

Wait, the ball isn't snapped yet! What if we don't fix identity or disappear it? What if it is transitory, as transitory as time, an impermanency within impermanency? If all is relationality, then identity, too is relational. If all is in dynamic movement, then identity too is in dynamic movement. So too is the natural attention of the "terms," that's us, in our organisms, in movement, our senses, our feelings, our thinking, within an everchanging environment responding to what is in the present

DOI: 10.1057/9781137300577

situation. What about contact at the organism/environment boundary? Let's go there, make that figural.

At a soccer game, we don't always follow the ball, even as a player, and most people in the stadium are not on the field. A fan goes to the game and certainly watches the ball, but that's not all there is. There are the particular figures that naturally arise, cohere into unities, and then go back into the background as other things in the environment become salient.

At one moment, putting ketchup on your hot dog is figural, then you take a bite, and even if you are also watching the game, you are also eating. So, no figure is fully attended, each a more blurry part of a weaker, but still whole gestalt. At another moment, when the ball gets closer to the goal, you become more absorbed in the game, following the ball more closely, the hot dog is put down, and we say, the game is getting exciting, but it is we who are excited by the interest and natural absorption we have in the game at that moment when the figure of "trying to score" becomes clear, bright and unified, and everything else submerges into ground, emptying it.

At another moment, the ball is back toward the center of the field and the figure changes to needing to use the restroom, then there is the navigating through the stands. On the field, a player also moves attentional focus, not always on the ball, not always potentiated by the two goals. At one moment, a player is thinking about a hamstring pull as a quick turn causes pain, at another moment, attention moves to a familiar pattern of movement on the field, and action is taken to thwart an anticipated kick to goal, the pain receding.

When the game is over, an overall figure emerges, it was "exciting" or "boring," depending on the moments of natural connection to, absorption in the play, the clarity and detail of the figures that emerged from the ground, for you and perhaps for others, during the game. These are times of spontaneous concentration that bring with them a sense of excitement, interest, and vitality (Perls, Hefferline, and Goodman, 1951).

Identity too, need not be fixed. It can come and go and change over time as what becomes salient, figural, changes across the situations of our lives. What once was important, is no longer, even moment to moment. We respond and are responding in every moment within the situation. If someone wants to make a story out of it, let them, but wait until its over, at least to see how it turns out, I mean, all stories have an end, and you never know until death. In the meantime...

What is happening now? The hand is on the ground. We are waiting for the snap of the ball. He spits on your hand. You flinch. A flag is thrown. You remember.

> I: And why do you think you remembered this moment?
>
> S: I think I remember that moment because I hadn't been playing football for very long. I think that was the first time that I actually experienced somebody being horrible for no reason. You know, I was young, I thought it was, it was just a game to me, and I wasn't serious about anything yet; I was in the fourth grade. So I think for the first time, that was when I saw somebody just be – it was almost like injustice. I saw a bunch of wrongdoings going on and everybody kind of turning their back, you know. Judges were rigged, people playing were rigged. I just, I thought it was crazy that people would just be so mean. Mean.

If identity is a story about yourself, one you learned in another moment, and that moment is no longer there, but you carry it with you as fixed, as identity, are you staring?

> I: And has this moment influenced how you think about yourself?
>
> S: In the long run, I think so.
>
> I: Can you say how?
>
> S: I just have a huge problem with not saying what's on my mind and I do a lot, I don't say anything that's on my – I don't say the things that are on my mind. And I don't know. I just think that moment had something to do with teaching me – I think it was just one of those defining moments. I did not do or say anything when that kid spit on my hand.

So, he does this a lot. The point is he's *not* doing now what he says he always does, but he doesn't see this. He *is* saying what is on his mind now. There is no judgment about this at all. We all can do whatever "this" is a lot, and to focus on narrative as identity means we are carrying around that "this" a lot and that may be shifting contact with what is happening in this moment to a narrowed version based on what happened before; now "terms" of our own making.

The flag is thrown. Flags are images of unity, of that which transcend time, of values, of identity held across time. We follow a flag in war, even if no longer carried high on horseback, we raise it in the morning and lower it at night. Flags fly half-mast when someone has died. Flags are draped then carefully folded in remembrance of great sacrifice. Flags are connected to death. So are we. Flags move with the moment, in the wind.

DOI: 10.1057/9781137300577

Why do we destroy, even a game, with a spit? Why not let go of staring at identity for fear of getting lost in a chaotic ground? We won't get lost; things might just happen that we don't prefer, but that happens anyway. There will always be destruction, each figure is destroyed before there is a new gestalt, a new figure. At the core of deconstruction is momentary creative reconstruction. Why not use this moment of the here and now actuality at the contact boundary of organism/environment, as the context for awareness, for choice, for change?

Set for the ... awareness of choice ... of responsibility ... of being here and now ...

I *was* a Y man.

DOI: 10.1057/9781137300577

3
Death

Abstract: *There are three moments in this chapter:* Question mark, Everything... lost its context, *and* Just pure joy. *Each moment describes an experience in relation to the death of a close family member, a baby, a brother, and a mother. The interpretive analysis of the moments addresses issues including the meaning of death, the ongoing experience of loss, chance, recognition, duality, and the experience of time. These moments are interpreted unto themselves without external sources.*

Forrest, Kelly. *Moments, Attachment and Formations of Selfhood: Dancing with Now.* Basingstoke: Palgrave Macmillan, 2013. DOI: 10.1057/9781137300577.

Question mark

> [I]t's going to be he's in an incubator, my family is surrounding me, the doctors have told us that he doesn't have much time left to live and we all kind of waited around for him to pass away. And I remember looking up at the monitor, 'cause it had his vital signs going down, down, down and then all of a sudden question mark. I knew, that question mark, you know okay, you've been told your baby's going to die. The question mark means your baby died. But I saw that question mark and I'm like what does that mean? What does that mean, you know? I remember that being significant, the death.

Life and death is a basic duality of which each of us is a part. What is death? What does it mean? The doctor knows there's not much time left to live, so there is a "waiting around" for the time of passing, the time of passing away. There is a monitor, an instrument that is specifically built to observe and transmit the signs of life, the vital signs, to others. This monitor is a machine. It has wires hooked up to another machine, an incubator, in which a baby is breathing, sensing, living, be-ing. Yet, too, the baby is passing a-way. Does the baby know? What way is this be-ing passing? What way are the others be-ing? They are "surround-ing," thus, they are exist-ing in space, relat-ing to one another in space. They are "wait-ing," that is they are engaged in an activity of wait-ing, waiting, for a future happening that is too occur soon, there is not much time left to live, so they are waiting for a death that is foreseen to soon occur.

What is the nature of this waiting? They are waiting "around." Here the a-round parallels the sur-round. There is an encircling quality to this waiting. Are they encircling the incubator or each other in space? Is the incubator accessible from all sides, so that the baby is experienc-ing this surround-ing and wait-ing around?

There is a remembrance of "looking up." In the waiting, then, there is an implied looking down. Is this a spatial necessity, that the incubator is lower than eye level? There is no indication in the waiting that there is an observing of the baby. The baby is absent except for its "passing away." They have been told the baby is "going to die." What is the nature of this go-ing? In the implied looking down, what is this be-ing see-ing? How will each of us meet the moment of our go-ing?

We know the biological gender of the baby, referred to as "he." Gender is a basic duality within culture. So much is defined, structured, and codified by gender. What do we know in this moment of be-ing, that this

DOI: 10.1057/9781137300577

baby is biologically a "he?" Is this be-ing also he-ing? Is there a he-ing at this age for this be-ing? Whose he-ing is it? His whole life already predicted by this he-ing of his be-ing. Whatever inherentness this category has in culture, at this moment, the monitor is showing that this be-ing has vital signs that are going "down, down, down." In looking up, there is a message of down, another duality.

Amidst this looking up at down, something occurs "all of a sudden." From where does this all of suddening source occur? There is a ground of something abiding, in time, staying, living, not dying, a sense of things moving along known dimensions, not swerving erratically to a qualitatively different realm, bringing "all of a sudden" a "question mark."

This question mark is already known. It is phrased in the past tense, "I knew." To know denotes awareness or knowledge. The question mark is the mark of a question. What is the question that is known? Or, is it the mark of an unknown question that is known? The meaning of the mark of the unknown question has been "told." The mark "means your baby died." What is happening to the questioning with the mark of meaning? What does the mark of meaning do to experiencing? Does it keep us questioning or end it? Another duality or is it duality-ing?

I: And why do you think you remembered that moment?

S: That was the moment that there was no turning back, he was gone, he was dead, there's no resuscitating him. I couldn't bring my baby back at that point.

I: And is that moment consistent or inconsistent with how you think about your self?

S: I think it's consistent

I: Can you say how?

S: Because even though rationally I knew that the question mark meant that he was dead, I still was like why, what does that mean? And even though I see something as real and tangible, I say what does that mean? I might know the answer but maybe I'm either trying to think about it too much or trying to find something bigger maybe.

Everything ... lost its context

Probably the first one that comes to mind is when I found my brother. He had passed away, so. I just, I went into his room to get him up and I was 15 at the time. And he just, he was just sitting on the corner and he had his

DOI: 10.1057/9781137300577

shirt on top of his head. He was profoundly autistic, so that's normal for him. And everything just seemed to be in slow motion. I could not wrap my mind around what was going on. I just remember freezing and being just – like I couldn't make time move. I just felt enveloped by that.

I: Is there anything else you'd like to add to your description of that moment?

S: I felt like I was underwater. It felt like I had lost all my sense of gravity like I literally really have gone down Alice's hole. Like everything had lost its context. Yeah.

What is context? The part of the word "con" usually denotes a "withing" aspect. Text generally refers to some representation of written language. The context are those parts of the written statement that appear before or after some specific word or passage that influences meaning.

What is the context of experience? It must be those aspects of experience that surround a particular experience that influences one's experiencing of that particular experience. But, isn't that particular experience also an experiencing? Or is there a difference between an experience and experiencing? What demarcates experiencing as surrounding experiencing from particular experiencing?

In this case, the particular experience is coming into the room and finding your brother passed away. The experience is of being "in slow motion," of not being able to "wrap my mind around what was going on," of "freezing," not being able to "make time move," and feeling "enveloped by that." The passage is in the past tense. This is understandable as the moment is being remembered. Yet, there is an instance in the text that refers to present tense activity, of "freezing," yet that too is appropriately contexted within the past, I "remember."

The past experience is added to with more descriptors of past tense experiencing, that of what it "felt like." Like has many uses in the English language, but here it is used as a simile. The experience felt like "I was underwater," "I had lost all my sense of gravity," and "literally really have gone down Alice's hole." There is a summary of this as well on a semantic level, "like everything had lost its context." The feeling is past, it "felt like I was," "felt like I had lost," and "like I literally, really have gone down." Wait, *have* gone down, I really literally have gone down – it *felt* like I literally really *have* gone down – felt, past tense, have, present tense. I felt in the past something that is continuing into the present, but then wouldn't that be it *feels* like I *have* gone down Alice's hole? Or, if all was in the past, wouldn't one say, it *felt* like I really *had* gone down?

DOI: 10.1057/9781137300577

Is this the source of the experiencing of the feeling that "everything had lost its context?" This is a subtle cue of dissociation reflected in language, the blurring of past and present. Such nuanced blurrings signal a current experience of temporal discontinuity within what is normally a linear past–present continuity. Here, in language, is a sign of "incoherence" that is talked about in narrative psychotherapy, one that says this identity, this self is less than coherent.

Yet, what does the person know of their present experiencing during the interview?

> I: And then this is the last question. What was your experience during this interview sharing your moments that matter?
>
> S: Well, I definitely had a lot of flooding and trying not to dissociate too phenomenally, just – I think for all of these moments, they are present for me a lot anyway. And I don't think that I typically like really – when I think about them, I don't think about them in detail, such as this opportunity, so. A little anxiety. Definitely today. Yeah.

There is a much deeper incoherence than the one this interviewee is aware of as an ongoing struggle, the one that is willingly engaged as part of this interview process, that is being experienced, being handled, away from the conversation, away from the interviewer's knowledge. A profound loss has been experienced, no, right there, that's the problem. The profound loss is *being* experienced; its past occurrence, the death, and its current consequence, intermingle. It is this past–present experiencing that must be healed through bringing the language back into coherence, so that the listener doesn't discern, become disoriented within the speaker's temporal infractions. No! This is how this be-ing is experience-ing the loss in the moment, in the actual here and now. What is being dissociated is the removal of that experience-ing from the conversation. This person is "trying not to dissociate too phenomenally." Yet, they say nothing of this during the conversation. It is only because the person was directly asked about their experiencing that we know of their experiencing.

The stronger dissociation here is what the context of the conversation, of being social, requires of the person who is experience-ing loss, not who has experience-ed a loss. When directly asked about their experience, the person doesn't dissociate. Rather, they tell us that they were "trying not to dissociate." Who is more dissociated here from what is actually going on during the conversation, the speaker or the listener? Dissociation is difficult to define, but in its broadest

DOI: 10.1057/9781137300577

understanding, the term reflects a separation where an integration is expected. What is the expectation of experiencing following a loss – there it is again – *following* a loss; so easily is the current experience placed into the past.

Conversations in interaction are a context which require a whole host of inhibitions regarding experiencing and expressing of experiencing. Loss is just one example that is, perhaps, more salient because it challenges the "normal" temporal ordering of events. Is it normal to have a life without loss, without movement of temporality, or is it normal to hold onto order in order to distance one's self from perceiving disorder?

What is the current experincing of telling about a loss? Generally, we don't know, we don't say, we just talk about what happened. Do we really know what the ordering of experienc-ing is? Have you asked anyone lately what their current actual in-the-moment here and now experiencing is? What is yours? Is there ever really a past tense of experiencing? Everything really has lost its contexting. It is good to listen to someone who's been there.

I: Has this moment influenced your thinking, feeling, or behavior in any way?

S: Yes

I: Can you say how?

S: It really caused a lot of soul searching I guess in terms of evaluating what I was doing in my life as things unfold and kind of this sense of like – I'm not describing it very well. It's definitely one of those sort of significant emotional events you can just sort of – it's one of those things where you always think of yourself in terms of before and after. It's a clear marker, you know, it's one of those points at which everything has to change, everything does change ... It amplified ... very existential questions, who I am and what am I doing here.

...

I: And do you think this moment will influence you in the future?

S: I think it's likely, yes.

I: And can you say how?

S: I just get a sense that its capacity to change me isn't done yet. As I go through life and try to continue to figure things out, it's sort of, I always sort of come back to that piece where everything blew up. I do continue to think about it in terms like, you know, carefully laid plans and the path you lay out for yourself that can be blown to smithereens in a nanosecond and nothing can be the same.

DOI: 10.1057/9781137300577

Just pure joy

> The first moment that comes to my mind is when my mother was dying of cancer and I had been, I had to go deliver a paper, and I was out of the country. And I came back and as it turned out, less than a week before she died. And I walked into the room and the moment that stands out to me is when she saw me walk in the room. And the look on her face and the way she opened her hands and acknowledged my presence – she couldn't talk. She was at that point where she was fading very fast. And that probably took less than five seconds. That moment. And boy, that – yeah, that stand, that really stands out to me. Very emotional.

I: Can you describe for me that five second moment of experience?

S: It was recognition. It was a moment of recognition from – and there was a moment of connection, a spark between us. Because I was afraid she wouldn't even know I was there. And at the minute I walked in the room and I walked over to her bed and I said hey momma, I'm here. I think before – I'm trying to remember; it's been a long time ago, but I think that she sensed me walk in the room. You know how you know somebody's footsteps? There were other people in the room. And I think that she somehow some way knew that it was me before I even said anything. And just that she barely opened her eyes. And it wasn't a look as much as it was a feeling. It was just boom, you know, I was right there.

I: Can you articulate the beginning and the end of the moment? There's this moment that you're saying was about five seconds long. And I'm wondering if you can articulate when, you know, the actual moment.

S: Hm. It was joy. It makes me cry just to think about it, but it was joy. It was an absolute sense of joy. 'Cause I was so afraid that she was going to be gone by the time I got there, and she was still there and conscious enough to know that I was there. That just, that was just, it was just pure joy. I don't know what else to do, I don't know how else to describe it.

There it is, in the midst of all the describing, all the contexting, all the orientation for the listener, there, behind, within the narrative surround, is the source of the remembrance of the moment, the moment itself, the feeling of joy. Without the further queries, the joy remains implicit in the conversation.

I: And why do you think you remembered that moment?

S: There was so much hanging on it, you know. There was so much hanging on that moment. If I walked in the room and she was unconscious or if I walked in the room and she had already been gone. So it was,

DOI: 10.1057/9781137300577

> there was a lot of anticipation and a lot of stress and, you know, just a lot of fear inside of me and a lot of hope that she was still there, that I would get to say goodbye to her, you know. So it was really intense. It was very intense.

Here is chance irrationally intervening in life. Exactly chance that is the enemy, chance that science has to work so hard to make go away, to predict, to control, the fear, the hope, the intensity of chance... and what does it allow? Just pure joy. Maybe there's more to chance than we think.

DOI: 10.1057/9781137300577

Part III
Responding to Narrative Psychology

Abstract: *This section summarizes the narrative turn in psychology in relation to identity practices and describes the two central critiques of the traditional "big story" approach to narrative identity based on its privileging of a particular view of self, one that is coherent, autonomous, and retrospectively focused, rather than multivoiced, relational, and centered in present interaction. The chapter sets forth the argument that the critiques are too limited in their challenge to the link between narrative coherence and healthy identity formation.*

Forrest, Kelly. *Moments, Attachment and Formations of Selfhood: Dancing with Now*. Basingstoke: Palgrave Macmillan, 2013. DOI: 10.1057/9781137300577.

Narrative psychology is guided by two grand images, that of *homo faber*, "man-the-maker," and *homo politicus*, "man-as-citizen" (Niebuhr, 1963). These two images are described in Niebuhr's *The Responsible Self*. This work is well known within theological and philosophical ethics and is grounded within the philosophy of symbolic forms.

> [The human] is a being who grasps and shapes reality, including the actuality of his own existence, with the aid of great images, metaphors, and analogies. These are partly in his conscious mind and in the social language that he tends to take them for granted as forms of pure reason. They are, indeed, forms of reason, but of historic reason. Thus man thinks of things anthropomorphically, or mechanomorphically, or mathematico-morphically, without always being aware that his patterns are not copies of the reality to which he reacts but products of an art of knowing in which subject and object interact. His conceptual systems, accordingly, are largely abstractions from his symbolic forms. (p. 61)

In the quest to know self, the most common symbol Niebuhr discerns within the Western world is that of the maker. We are makers fashioning reality, like so many artists and craftsmen, towards some good, some ideal. "Man is the being who makes himself – though he does not do so by himself – for the sake of a desired end" (p. 49). How often do we act with some future state of affairs in mind? Whether as individuals, groups, or nations, we act teleologically, directing our gaze toward the future and taking steps in light of our goals. Freedom in this context means the right of self-determination, to choose which means to which ends.

In narrative psychology, the maker image predominates within a paradigm of self and identity construction. In the 1980s, narrative was turned to as the root metaphor in psychology (Sarbin, 1986). Old ways of thinking about human beings, as objects to be dissected in the laboratory of impersonal inquiry, the whole of the human seen in parts in images of the mechanical, spatial, and energy, were worn out. New metaphors were searched for to enliven the field. The answer came from history, or more precisely meta-history. History was a form of storytelling. Yes, stories would provide the antidote to the inanimate decontextualized, positivist images of the human being. Stories were deeply contextual and relational; history and narrative were siblings, both cut from the same cloth. History and narrative would breathe life into events, the past revivified in the present.

And, there would be order. Narrative organized experience within constant change. Situations were structured, actors positioned, and none

DOI: 10.1057/9781137300577

of it need be mechanistically linear; the plot was a liberating structure, even if appearing chaotic to those dwelling in the order, predictability, and causality of positivist conditioning. The return of the subjective, the author, was also hailed. The "vague but indispensable construct, the self" (Sarbin, 1986, p. 18) can imagine the future and reconstruct the past, making narration possible. Here, activity was returned to the self; no longer relegated to object status.

This call was taken up as narrative became, not just an organizing principle, a way to understand how human beings "think, perceive, imagine and make moral choices" (Sarbin, 1986, p. 8), but as the fundamental process in the formation of identity and sense of self: narrative answered the question, "Who am I?" Thus, narrative tellings are viewed, not just as the building blocks of identity formation, but as identity, as self (McAdams, 1993). Our stories are the myths we live by, the myths we are.

In linguistics, Labov's (Labov, 1972; Labov and Waletzky, 1967) discovery of a common structure in non-literary narrative fueled the emergence of narrative inquiry of personal stories in psychology and across the social sciences. The analysis of narrative offered a privileged entrance into the study of identity and self. The privileging of subjective voice was widely welcomed as the limitations of the positivist based approaches that foregrounded the rational, impersonal, and mechanistic had eroded confidence in the capacity of science to say something meaningful about human beings.

As the metaphor of narrative was grounded in the notion that humans perceive the world in narrative form or that the act of narrating gives order, meaning, and structure to experience, narrative became not just a practice for constructing identity, but a prescription for health, to ward off the chaos of an unordered and disorienting world (e.g. Carr, 1986; Sarbin, 1986; Bruner, 1986).

In the same time frame of the ascendance of narrative in empirical psychology, the purposing of narrative as a healing agent gained purchase from psychotherapeutic work. In particular, those professional psychologists and researchers working in the field of trauma described the effects on healthy functioning that lack of coherence between aspects of self – behavior, affect, sensation, and knowledge – wrought (Herman, 1992).

Recently, Bamberg (2011) has articulated three challenges that identity formation processes face. He describes these challenges in terms of "dilemmatic spaces." Identity formation must navigate constancy and change over time, between sameness and difference at any given point

DOI: 10.1057/9781137300577

in time, and manage agency within the bidirectional relation between person and world.

Trauma disrupts all three spaces. Particularly within conditions of chronic trauma, fragmentation and integration are polar processes (Herman, 1992).

> Fragmentation in consciousness prevents the ordinary integration of knowledge, memory, emotional states, and bodily experience. Fragmentation in the inner representations of self prevents the integration of identity. Fragmentation in the inner representations of others prevents the development of a reliable sense of independence within connection. (Herman, 1992, p. 107)

The basis for these fragmentations is the adaptive function of attempting to preserve relationship in the face of trauma (Herman, 1992). Disruptions in the normal regulation of bodily and emotional states together with alterations in self-perception, relations with others, and in systems of meaning are the effects of chronic or "complex" trauma that can last into adulthood (Herman, 1992).

In this context, it is understandable that narrative, with its order and meaning-making function, would be graped, not only as a vehicle for stabilizing the disregulating and disorienting effects of big "T" trauma, but as a way to organize life within the everday little "t" trauma that the rapid pace and changing conditions of modernity entails. Narrative serves as a protective splint for the self, holding it together and steady amidst the disruptions and discontinuities that trauma presents, in all its guises, in all three dilemmatic spaces.

As narrative inquiry has progressed, however, what was hailed as an innovative and liberating approach to the study of identity has become the object of interrogation and sustained critique. One of the main critiques in narrative identity research has come from Bamberg and Georgakopoulou (Bamberg, 1997; Georgakopoulou, 2007). They view traditional "big story" narrative as privileging certain kinds of subjectivities, autonomous, self-contained selves, certain types of structured accounts, life stories or landmark events with temporal, causal, and thematic coherence, and a particular temporal orientation toward understanding of past happenings. Other types of voices, relational voices, and other types of structures, dynamic, interactional structures with a temporal focus on the here and now, termed "small stories," are revealed to have been marginalized or silenced within the traditional Labovian frame.

DOI: 10.1057/9781137300577

The call is to add "small stories" to the discussion on narrative identity, exploring the silenced end of the narrative dimensions, stories with multiple co-tellers versus one active teller, low versus high tellability, embeddedness in the local context versus detachment from the surrounding activity, an uncertain, fluid moral stance versus a certain and constant one, and an open-ended temporal and/or spatial organization versus a closed, causal ordering (Georgakopoulou, 2007; Ochs and Capps, 2001).

These non-canonical narratives in interaction are viewed as offering insight into how selves position themselves locally within an ongoing interpersonal dialogue and the context of their occurrence. In this approach, there is an understanding that selves are relational beings, less coherent and integrated than the image of self conveyed through traditional narrative. Relational selves are subject to the judgment of others; there are inconsistencies and contradictions in the ways selves are narrated across local contexts. The field of social psychology as a whole testifies to the influence of local situational effects on identities within groups. Yet, even within the small story approach, self and identity remain largely within the constructivist frame, that of the maker image, although with an enlivened emphasis on identity's interactive co-construction in temporally present local contexts.

A second important critique of the traditional image of narrative identity targets the link between coherence and identity more directly, specifically positing a multivoiced self, inspired by Bakhtin's polyphonic metaphor (Hermans, Kempen, and Van Loon, 1992). In this view, there is no requirement for an integrated and unified self and no need to construct such a unity. Rather, the self is multivoiced, a "dynamic multiplicity of relatively autonomous I-positions" and, rather than integration, the focus is placed on the process of positioning between selves (Hermans, 2001, p. 248).

Dialogue is the field of activity wherein selves (internal and external) meet in the "processes of negotiation, cooperation, opposition, conflict, agreement, and disagreement" (p. 253). In this view, the understanding of identity/self shifts from the work of construction for some desired end to the process of regulating the tension between multiplicity and harmony through positioning. There is also a temporal shift to the present whereby selves position themselves and select voice within an ongoing dynamic situated present.

This approach finds its home within the second grand image identified by Niebuhr (1963), that of "citizen." Here, the body, emotions, sensations,

DOI: 10.1057/9781137300577

and impulses become salient aspects of self that, unlike the material of a craftsman, are not chosen, but are given us. To these aspects of living, we are more as administrator to citizens than artist to material: life is like politics more than art or techne. We live, as Freud articulated, our urges, fears, angers, love together with sources of punishment and guilt. We come to awareness within values, rules and laws, parental repressions and permissions, community and cultural ethos, religious sanctions, all the shalts and shalt nots. Yet, unlike Freud, the multiplicity of voice, of body, is not repressed, it is positioned, regulated in a dynamic tension of "multiplicity seeking unity or a unity diversifying" into various roles as the challenges of the administrative self (p. 54).

What systems of thought do we work within, the thoughts that govern our actions? To which laws do we adhere, to which do we rebel? Here, there is understanding that the body self is not under control, as the maker image, the artist choosing his materials, would necessitate. Rather, the political image is used, the image is of governing, inward self-regulation and external rule, each an administrative-self consenting to some discipline, to some law, and rebelling against others.

And what of the ultimate fate of our lives, what control over that have we? In the citizen image, there is an acceptance of chance happening, thus, for the citizen, the goal is not primary as it is for the maker, whether it be articulated as peace, happiness, prosperity or something else. Rather, it is the process of living under the rule of justice that reigns, that which ostensibly affords each a voice, a place of existence in the community of selves. The good is subordinated to the right. The debate can go on as to which law to follow, the law of nature, law of God, legislative action, judicial law, but each is under the same image, the symbol of citizen. The self's agency is administrative, obedient and legislative, law-abiding, and law-making. Within the self, likewise, the image is one of self-governance; what is the law of my life?

In Hermans' description, there is some ambiguity regarding how these dialogic processes occur. Various positions are taken up based on situational or cultural factors. People are said to "exchange knowledge" and the space of dialogue is seen as places for "question and answer, for agreement and disagreement" (Hermans, 2001, p. 259). People construct meanings, but within the constraints of voice positions organized and colored by social position. Cultural and structural processes are interiorized as voice positioning is governed by social definitions, expectations, and prescriptions raising issues of dominance and subordination, while

DOI: 10.1057/9781137300577

simultaneously individuals organize their lives in accordance or in opposition to these positions. What is clear from Herman's view is the open acceptance of multiplicity within selves and a focus on positioning of self in an inner and outer community of selves.

Thus, both major critiques of traditional narrative identity emphasize the relational nature of selves and are chipping away at the link between narrative coherence and healthy identity formation. This is work in the right direction because there is understanding that partial views of human experiencing, of necessity, silence other ways of experiencing. They are also pointing to a present-centered approach for exploring identity practices. Yet, the challenge does not go far enough.

Why not?

DOI: 10.1057/9781137300577

4
Language Isn't Everything

Abstract: *Highlighting research and theory from infant and adult attachment, this chapter argues that narrative coherence is not necessarily indicative of coherence of mind and body. The infant and adult attachment literature is described and used as evidence for the argument that language is sourced in affect and action. Particular attention is given to the adult attachment interview which reveals that narratives of self can have the appearance of coherence even as they serve as self-regulatory mechanisms, displacing immediate experience in the present moment with meanings based on past conditioning.*

DOI: 10.1057/9781137300577

The first reason is that language isn't all of human experiencing. Research coming out of areas at the intersection of psychology and psychoanalysis, including attachment and infant development, are demonstrating that language is sourced from a much broader and richer base within affect and action (BCPSG, 2010). It's turning out that:

> language and symbolic forms of meaning are intrinsically grounded in … early forms of implicitly represented relational experience. (BCPSG, 2010, p. 147)

Although there is a deep infusion of implicit with explicit ways of knowing, implicit processes are placed in a new light. Counter to earlier understandings, implicit ways of knowing are not "primitive" or "impoverished events" in comparison to the more explicit, reflective semiotic processes, nor are they "limited to … impersonal realms of procedural memory" such as riding a bicycle, as described in cognitive psychology (p. 147). Rather, implicit knowledge is broader in scope than explicit knowledge "at all ages" and "continues to grow in breadth and elaboration with age" (p. 147). Implicit knowing is "highly complicated knowledge involving affective responses, expectations, and thoughts (p. 147)."

To give an illustration, I use an example from the Boston Change Process Study Group (2010) regarding the interaction between a young depressed mother and her 18-month toddler during a home observation.

> [T]he mother is sitting on the couch and her son is also on the couch sitting a foot or two away drinking from his bottle. She is sitting stiffly in the far corner of the sofa and staring into space, smoking a cigarette with one hand and resting her other arm along the back of the couch in the direction of her son. Her toddler finishes his bottle and stands up on the couch, bouncing up and down for a minute or two. Then he pauses before flopping over onto his mother's lap. At this point, without moving her stiff and remote arms, she jerks her head toward him and barks, "I told you not to jump on the couch!" (p. 146)

Later interactions during the same home observation show the infant walking up to his mother and "reach[ing] out his hand toward her knee, only to pull it away suddenly before actually touching her." These interactions are used to illustrate how the mother uses "intense affects" to "shut down certain forms of dialogue with her infant (e.g., affectionate physical contact)" and how the infant then "incorporates" this, not in content form, but in implicit process form "as a part of his own attempts to shut down those same forms of discourse within" (p. 146). The learned implicit

DOI: 10.1057/9781137300577

process is "hate for attachment bids and profound resistance to reaching out to others for help." Such implicit relational knowing influences interactions with others and is "foundational" to subjectivities (p. 150).

The moments presented in this project are, I believe, sourcing in memory particularized enactments of implicit ways of relational knowing and most reflect a continuing influence on the linkages to constructed symbolic meaning regarding self and identity. The feeling of unworthiness and unlovability expressed in the *Black rocking chair* moment stands out in this regard. There, the woman is loved by her husband and children, but does not feel the love that is there. The grounding of explicit processes in implicit relational knowing is palpably expressed as the disappointed expectation of love linked to a judgment of unworthiness of self sustains the sadness. Similarly, the momentary experience in *Set for the ... snap* is characterized as a defining moment for self, in how self relates to others. Even in the more benign example of the *Wonderful sad monkey*, where a connection to self is disavowed, there are indicators of implicit relational knowing, the willingness to approach, the desire to bridge a felt distance from another being, the desire to hug, and the sense of communication through the eyes. Could our remembered moments carry implicit conditioned intentions, expectations, or assumptions, that as vows, are held as truth?

Important to note is that not all represented meaning has a verbal, symbolic, or imagistic form (BCPSG, 2010). Implicit relational knowing is a form of representation, of knowing, but it does not imply a symbolic process. Instead, its base is in affect and action. It is "crucial," however, not to assume that implicit knowledge is non-verbal or preverbal (p. 153, citing Lyons-Ruth, 1999). As in the adult attachment interview, which is discussed hereinafter, implicit ways of knowing can be revealed through language, but for this, one needs to read "between the lines" for the underlying "rules" or "syntax" of interaction, including any defensive distortions to the open expression of affective relatedness within relationships (p. 153).

If one reads the *Black rocking chair* moment in this way, the affect and action basis in the language reveals the implicit inner resistance toward reaching out toward love and allowing it in. Think also of those times when you are trying to express something that is just so difficult to put into words. Generally, it is when you are trying to synthesize a whole array of feelings and thoughts that are all there, but just beneath the surface of articulation. As such, the explicit, language based system is

DOI: 10.1057/9781137300577

a tool for communicating what is an "exceedingly rich and elaborated," "primary relational meaning system" (p. 145).

This critique of narrative psychology has a foundation in the sourcing of language in implicit experience, in action and affect. Therefore, a relatively detailed overview of the attachment literature is provided to ground the reader in a rigorous evidence based source for the argument.

At its core, attachment is based in action and affect, not in language. Attachment refers to the phenomenon that when we are alarmed, we not only run away from what is alarming, but "[w]e run TO someone, usually a person" (Hesse and Main, 2000). John Bowlby, in a trilogy of work (1969/1982, 1973, 1980), was the first to synthesize literature from differing fields, including evolutionary theory, ethology, and cognitive psychology, and propose that infants are evolutionarily adapted to instinctively initiate and maintain contact with primary caregiving figures, particularly in situations of stress or external threat, in order to increase the chances for survival. Bowlby proposed that attachment could be understood as an instinctive complex behavioral control system that evolved to maintain an infant within a certain distance from the caregiver as a protection against predation and other survival related dangers (Bowlby 1969/1982). When there are clues to danger in the internal or external environment during the first years of life, the attachment system activates and the infant seeks proximity to the caregiver (Bowlby, 1969/1982).

To gain a sense of what Bowlby (1969/1982) proposed regarding the attachment behavioral system, it will be helpful to begin with a simple control system. A simple control system is a fixed action pattern. A fixed action pattern is a "structured pattern of movement" that is different from a reflex because the threshold for its activation, rather than holding constant, varies with the state of the organism (Bowlby, 1969/1982, p. 66). Once initiated, the highly stereotyped movements of fixed action patterns follow their course without much regard for what is occurring in the environment. More complicated control systems operate using feedback, working to reduce discrepancies between a set goal and current performance. A thermostat and the power steering on a car are examples of control systems that operate using set goals and environmental feedback. The difference between the two is that, in power steering, the set goal keeps changing, while for a thermostat, the set-goal is constant. Importantly, these set-goals, should not be viewed in terms of outcomes, rather, they are process goals. To illustrate, the set-goal of a power steering mechanism is to continuously bring the front wheels to align with the

DOI: 10.1057/9781137300577

position the driver sets and resets for the steering wheel, not to drive to a particular place. The set goal for the attachment behavioral system is to maintain a certain proximity to the caregiver. This is true even during times of relative safety as the infant needs to "at some level continually 'track' the physical and psychological accessibility of the primary attachment figure(s), whether or not attachment behavior is explicitly displayed at any given time" (Main, Hesse, and Kaplan, 2005, p. 253–254). During times of threat, the attachment system is dominantly activated in reference to other potentially competing behavioral systems. When the attachment behavioral system is dominant, the infant seeks to elicit closer contact with the caregiver using a repertoire of behavior, including looking, crying and locomotion. Upon reunion, the experience of danger dissipates as the caregiver comforts and reassures the infant. This allows the attachment system to move into the background and a second complex behavioral control system, labeled the exploratory system, to become dominantly active. Exploration requires the orientation of head and body toward objects of interest in the environment together with approach behavior toward such objects for further investigation (Bowlby, 1969/1982). The activation of the exploratory behavioral system is manifested by an infant who, following an experience of danger, returns to play.

The interaction of attachment and exploratory behavior in infants has been observed in the home and controlled laboratory settings (Ainsworth et al., 1978; Karen, 1998). Attachment status in infants can be reliably measured by 12 months of age using the laboratory procedure developed by Mary Ainsworth (1967), termed the strange situation. This method consists of a series of brief episodes which places the infant in increasingly stressful situations, including interacting with a stranger and being alone, followed in each case by a reunion with the mother or primary caregiver. Infants are classified as to their type of attachment based on their behavior during the separation and reunion episodes. The relative balance of the activation of the attachment and exploratory behavioral systems during this procedure differentiates infants regarding their attachment status. Infant behavior during the strange situation is not based on temperament, but rather is the result of the child-rearing environment (Main, Hesse, and Kaplan, 2005). Infants have been classified into three organized categories of attachment, secure, insecure-anxious avoidant, and insecure-anxious ambivalent/resistant.

Infants who are classified as secure show attentional flexibility during the strange situation episodes, being able to focus their attention on the

DOI: 10.1057/9781137300577

salient aspect of the unfolding episodes as they occur (Main, 2000; Main, Hesse, and Kaplan, 2005). Secure infants are distressed when the mother leaves, but are quickly, if not immediately soothed upon her return, and can thereafter resume their exploratory behavior with the toys in the room (Main, 2000). This fluid balancing of attachment and exploratory behavior in response to stressful situations – seeking proximity to the caregiver when distressed, being soothed, and then being able to return to play – has been linked with a history of interactions with a primary caregiver who has been predictably sensitive and responsive to an infant's attachment-related signals (Main, 2000; Ainsworth et al., 1978). In times of stress, these caregivers have assisted the infant to downregulate overarousal, minimize negative affect, and transition from negative to positive states (Tronick, 1989). In this way, the primary caregiver acts as a "safe haven" in times of distress and a "secure base" from which the infant can explore (Main, 2000).

These dyadic interactions with the caregiver are "centrally involved" in emotion regulatory processes and in cognitive appraisals regarding expectations of self and other, particularly during times of stress (Schore, 1996, p. 73; Schore, 1994). As they mature, secure infants can tolerate increasing levels of arousal and affect when the caregiver is not present, thus moving gradually from an external to a more internalized, self-generated, homeostatic regulatory capacity. In neurobiological terms, through experience-dependent fronto-limbic maturation, the infant gradually maintains a neurophysiological excitation–inhibition balance and is able to generate adaptive cognitive expectations in dynamic response to changing environmental stimulation. Secure infants are thus able to shift their attention flexibly to whatever presents itself in the moment because they have been enabled to dynamically self-regulate in response to the ebb and flow of life.

Not all infants, however, show attentional flexibility during the strange situation. Infants classified as insecure-anxious avoidant (anxious avoidant) and insecure-anxious ambivalent/resistant (anxious ambivalent) maintain self-regulation through the organized, but inflexible use of attention (Main, 2000). The attention of anxious-avoidant infants is inflexibly focused on the environment. Even during the most stressful episode of the strange situation, being left alone in an unfamiliar room for three minutes, anxious-avoidant infants continue to play with the toys (Main, 2000). When the mother returns, these infants do not seek contact with her, but rather may look away, withdrawing from the mother's approach, and continue to focus on the toys in the room. With

DOI: 10.1057/9781137300577

anxious avoidant infants, "there is no dramatic rise and fall of emotion, no crisis followed by a happy ending. Indeed, it appears as if nothing has happened at all" (Main, 2000, p. 1072). However, something definitely has happened. The play of anxious-avoidant infants is impoverished compared to that of secure infants (Main and Weston, 1982). Anxious avoidant infants cannot engage as intensely with the toys because they are significantly distressed at the physiological level during the strange situation episodes (Main, 2000; Sroufe and Waters, 1977; Spangler and Grossman, 1999; Dozier and Kobak, 1992). The attachment system of anxious avoidant infants is activated, however, these infants have learned not to express their distress through a history of dyadic interactions with a mother that has rejected their attachment overtures (Main, 2000; Ainsworth et al., 1978). These mothers show a pattern of interaction characterized by withdrawal, hesitancy, and a reluctance to organize or regulate infant behavior and attention (Main and Weston, 1982). Anxious avoidant infants have not been assisted in regulating the negative affect and arousal that is induced by environmental stress or by the parent's aversion to their attempts to initiate contact. Thus, these infants have learned to withdraw their attention from attachment-activating stimuli (the parent and the stress of separation) and focus on the inanimate environment in order to maintain behavioral organization (Main, 2000). Main suggests this infant avoidance also operates to reduce caregiver attention to the infant thereby decreasing potential situations of rejection (Main, Hesse, and Kaplan, 2005).

Insecure-anxious ambivalent infants likewise show an organized, attentional inflexibility; however, in this case, the infants focus their attention more rigidly, not on the inanimate environment, but on the attachment figure (Main, 2000). This attentional strategy is an adaptive response to a dyadic interaction history with a primary caregiver who has shown unpredictable responsiveness to the infant's attachment overtures, but not rejection. These infants show high levels of distress during the strange situation long after the mother returns, thus showing a hypervigilant attentional style or a failure to deactivate the dominance of the attachment system. The result is that these infants spend virtually no time exploring the toys in the room.

The insecure anxious infants are unable to use the primary caregiver as a safe haven in times of distress or as a secure base in times of safety (Main, Hesse, and Kaplan, 2005). Instead, the attachment and exploratory systems develop a bias toward seemingly exploratory (anxious

DOI: 10.1057/9781137300577

avoidant) or attachment behaviors (anxious ambivalent) during times of stress, and these biases require the infant to sacrifice attentional flexibility in the moment.

There is a fourth insecure classification, disorganized/disoriented, which is characterized, not by an organized shift of attention toward the environment or the attachment figure, but by the collapse or absence of an attentional strategy (Hesse and Main, 2006). During the strange situation, these infants show episodes of contradictory movement patterns, such as "rocking on the hands and knees following an abortive approach" to the parent or a disorientation to the present environment, such as freezing, stilling, or slowed motor movements (p. 1099). These anomalous behaviors, which occur briefly, are proposed to result from the infant being in a situation of "fright without solution" (p.1099). When alarmed, the attachment behavioral system activates and the infant seeks proximity to the caregiver. However, if the caregiver is the source of the alarm, the infant is placed in the paradoxical predicament of simultaneously running *to* and *away from* the source of fear.

Although initially researched in infancy, attachment processes operate from "the cradle to the grave" (Bowlby, 1979, p. 129). Longitudinal studies have established the relative intraindividual stability of attachment classification into adulthood and its interpersonal transmission across generations (Main, Hesse, and Kaplan, 2005; see Hesse, 1999). Attachment in older children and adults is assessed based on individual differences in mental representation or internal working models of attachment, rather than on non-verbal behavior.

An internal working model of attachment is defined as "a set of conscious and/or unconscious rules for the organization of information relevant to attachment and for obtaining or limiting access to that information, that is, to information regarding attachment-related experiences, feelings, and ideations" (Main, Hesse, and Kaplan, 2005 citing Main, Kaplan, and Cassidy, 1985, p. 66–67). Primary representations of attachment in internal working models are whether assistance can be expected in times of distress and how worthy the self is to receive assistance. These expectations are founded upon the interactional history with primary caregiver(s).

In adults and children over 10 years of age, internal working models of attachment can be assessed through language using the Adult Attachment Interview (AAI), (George et al., 1996; Hesse, 1999). The AAI is a 20 question semi-structured interview that assesses the speaker's

DOI: 10.1057/9781137300577

state of mind regarding attachment, rather than attachment to a specific person, as is assessed in the strange situation. As attachment processes operate largely implicitly (Bowlby, 1969/1982), the AAI is designed to capture these processes through the sequencing of the questions and the nature of the interview task.

The questions in the AAI are said to "surprise the unconscious" as they are structured to move, as the episodes in the strange situation, from less stressful to more stressful queries. For example, initially speakers are asked to provide general evaluative descriptions of childhood experiences with caregivers, but this is then followed by requests for specific illustrative memories that support these descriptions (Main, 2000). Speakers are also asked about significant separations from parents, losses due to death, and any rejecting, threatening or abusive behavior by parents. These experiences are particularly salient in attachment because they involve experiences of losing a parent or losing access to a parent when needed, thus activating the attachment behavioral system. Current relationships with parents are also queried.

As the AAI requires speakers to give specific experiences and evaluations at the semantic level of life histories, the interview provides many opportunities for speakers to contradict themselves or fail to provide support for their evaluations (for a review, see Hesse, 1999). This aspect of the AAI's structure foregrounds its focus on internal consistency, a component of coherence of transcript, that is a salient factor in coding for security/insecurity of attachment. The interview context also highlights the collaborative nature of the speaker's task. Taken together, the central task for a speaker in the AAI is to be able to present a coherent picture of one's attachment experiences and *simultaneously* be a collaborative partner in the interview context. The AAI requires speakers to describe and evaluate their attachment-related experiences in the context of an interview and its narrative analysis looks for internal consistency in the text of the transcript as well as the speaker's collaboration in the interview process.

The AAI was designed to capture the implicit operation of internal working models of speakers, models that developed from and are reflective of a process taking place in action and affect. This is the brilliance of the AAI, that the interview and its narrative analysis were developed based on the connection of language use of the adult to the behavioral patterns of mother-infant dyads in relational interaction during the strange situation. For example, a mother's discourse strategy in the AAI

DOI: 10.1057/9781137300577

highly correlates (70–80 per cent) with her infant's behavioral patterns in the strange situation, that is, how she and her infant interact, particularly upon reunion (for a review, see Hesse, 1999). This is true even when the AAI is given to the mother prior to the birth of her child. This is also the reason that longitudinal studies show similarly strong predictability between security assessed in infancy and secure/insecure statues into adulthood (Main, Hesse, and Kaplan, 2005; Sroufe et al., 2005).

The attachment literature reveals that language use is reflective of a process that is taking place implicitly in action and affect. The AAI is specifically designed to assess this link. Thus, it is not the construction of a coherent narrative, per se, that is correlated with secure attachment. Rather, the nature of coherence in the AAI is dependent on the structure of the interview, including its request for specific experiences as evidence for characterizations at the semantic level, and the need for speaker's responses to maintain relevancy to the interviewer's questions. This is the reason why discourse strategy rather than veridicality of content is salient for coding the interview. This is also a reason that verbal fluency, level of intelligence, and temperament do not correlate with AAI classification. Rather, security/insecurity of attachment is assessing the link between language and its implicit source in action and affect, a link that I would argue reflects a relative harmony/disharmony of mind with body.

The attentional flexibility the AAI is revealing is the speaker's ability to be present with immediate experience and responsive to the interviewer questions as attachment experiences are being discussed. The particular ways the speaker restricts the free flow of thoughts and feelings regarding attachment experiences and the active, fresh, in-the-moment monitoring of and reflecting on these thoughts and feelings determine attachment classification.

With this understanding of how coherence is assessed, AAI transcripts of low-risk, non-clinical populations are generally classified into one of four categories: secure/autonomous, dismissing, preoccupied, and unresolved. There is a fifth category of cannot classify that is more seen in high-risk, clinical populations.

Specifically, AAI coders evaluate inferred attachment-related experiences (love, rejection, neglect, involving/preoccupying, and pressure to achieve) in conjunction with the speaker's state of mind regarding those experiences (coherence, idealizing, derogating, lack of recall, anger, passivity, and fear of loss) (Main, Goldwyn, and Hesse, 2003). This information is then evaluated against a set of criteria for each of the three main

DOI: 10.1057/9781137300577

adult attachment classifications (secure/autonomous, dismissing, preoccupied). These classifications reflect differing ways individuals organize their thoughts and feelings regarding attachment experiences.

If the speaker reports loss of a loved one or an experience that meets the criteria for abuse, the coder also evaluates whether the speaker may be unresolved for the loss or abuse. Importantly, the veridicality of the reported experiences is irrelevant to the coding of the AAI transcript. It is the discourse strategy used by the speaker, rather than the content per se, that is assessed.

As with the non-verbal behavior of infants in the strange situation, secure/autonomous adults show a flexibility of attention that is manifested in their discourse strategy during the AAI (Main, 2000). Secure speakers are able to produce and freshly reflect on childhood memories, whether positive or negative, and, at the same time, are able to maintain collaborative discourse with the interviewer. The secure/autonomous status of primary caregivers is highly predictive of their infants' security during the strange situation (Hesse, 1999). However, as with the insecure infants, dismissing and preoccupied adults show an inflexibility of attention during the adult attachment interview (Main, 2000).

The transcripts of dismissing adults manifest a discourse strategy that inflexibly seeks to shift attention away from attachment-activating memories. These speakers' responses are relatively brief and convey a more positive image of childhood than they are able to support by specific illustrative childhood experiences. Thus, although the speakers can provide a coherent, if concise, narrative of their childhood, in the context of the AAI interview, these speakers present an overall incoherent picture of their attachment-related experiences.

Preoccupied speakers also produce transcripts that are incoherent regarding their experiences of attachment, but for different reasons. The discourse in these transcripts is sufficiently vague, irrelevant, angry, or fearful so that the speakers' absorption in their attachment-related experiences is interfering with their responsivity to the interviewer. Thus, in contrast to dismissing adults, preoccupied speakers inflexibly shift attention toward attachment-activating memories. Again, these transcripts may provide a coherent story of what has occurred, for example, how awful the parent is in specific ways, but this does not translate to coherence as assessed by the AAI. Rather, the preoccupied speakers' inability to flexibly regulate their attention reveals their reacting from past conditioning to what is affectively arising instead of being able, in the

DOI: 10.1057/9781137300577

moment, to note and regulate the affect while maintaining collaborative responding in the interview context.

Dismissing and preoccupied parental states of mind are predictive of infant attachment classification. A dismissing parental state of mind regarding attachment predicts insecure-anxious-avoidant infant behavior during the strange situation and a preoccupied parental state of mind predicts infant insecure-anxious-ambivalent/resistant attachment.

The next adult attachment classification is unresolved. Transcripts that are categorized as unresolved show brief collapses in attentional strategy during discussion of loss or abuse (for a review, see Hesse, 2000). These transcripts, which may otherwise manifest an organized secure/autonomous or insecure dismissing or insecure preoccupied discourse strategy through most of the interview, show lapses in the monitoring of discourse or reasoning specifically when discussing losses of significant attachment figures or abusive experiences by parents. These, sometimes brief, slips of attention within interview transcripts of unresolved parents are predictive of infant disorganization/disorientation during the strange situation.

The final category of adult attachment is cannot classify. This category indicates that no single state of mind regarding attachment predominates the interview. Thus, contradictory discourse strategies reflecting insecure styles, such as dismissing and preoccupied, can be reflected in one transcript. This category is relatively rare in low-risk samples and more prevalent in high-risk populations (see Hesse, 2000).

In summary, over the last two decades, the attachment literature is establishing the importance of early interactions with caregivers, based in affect and action, in the development of attentional flexibility as an important self-regulatory strategy that persists into adulthood when attachment-activating stimuli are present (Main, 2000). In optimal caregiving environments, attentional flexibility is developed through sensitive and responsive parental feedback to the infant's signals, thus allowing a fluid shifting of attention to what is salient in each moment. In non-optimal caregiving environments, the attentional flexibility of the infant is sacrificed to maintain self-regulation.

The attachment behavioral control system is relatively environmentally labile (Bowlby, 1969/1982). Thus, behavioral patterns of expectations of self-in-relation-to-other, which develop during the first years of life, are conditioned through the dyadic interactions the infant has had with primary caregivers, which are based in action and affect. Of particular

DOI: 10.1057/9781137300577

salience are those interactions occurring during times of fear, stress, or threat, as these are the times when proximity to a caregiver is most needed for protection (Ainsworth et al., 1978). The attentional strategies infants develop for self-regulation are adaptive to their ongoing attachment-based, dyadic, interactions.

In adulthood, the individual differences in attentional flexibility related to attachment reflect, at the representational level, differences in internal working models of attachment. These internal working models of attachment have self-regulatory implications for how individuals respond to stress, interpret emotionally salient stimuli, and regulate attention (Fonagy and Target, 2002; Calkins, 2004). Thus, what the AAI reveals is that language use is reflective of a self-regulatory function that can subordinate immediate experience in order to maintain a conditioned organization of self-in-relation. It is this self-organization that narrative coherence is maintaining, but it is doing so by sacrificing immediate experience together with an active, fresh, response to the evidence being remembered.

Before leaving the attachment overview, it is important here to note that I am not limiting my critique of narrative psychology for those persons who have insecure attachment. There are linguistic indicators of insecure attachment even within the secure category, although they are more mild. In addition, although I believe that attachment organizes much of our relations to self and others, there are socio-cultural structures, such as race, gender, sexual orientation, and socio-economic status that serve as sources for implicit relational knowing that lay more or less outside the realm of attachment experiences. I am providing the attachment literature to ground the reader in a rigorously researched evidence base specifically regarding the nature of the relationship between action, affect and language. For readers who are interested in current developments in the field of attachment, I would refer them to the *Handbook of Attachment* (Cassidy and Shaver, 2008).

The attachment literature offers important insights into the difficulties narrative psychologists have in establishing the link between narrative coherence and health benefits despite the intuitive appeal of the narrative coherence-health heuristic. It also assists in explaining why certain linguistic features of narratives can correlate with physical and mental health, yet at the same time leave researchers scratching their heads regarding the results (e.g. Ramírez-Esparaza and Pennebaker, 2006). As discussed earlier, the narrative analysis used to code the AAI does

DOI: 10.1057/9781137300577

not work in a linguistic vacuum, rather it is embedded in and derived from the deeper level of action and affect. Narrative psychologists may be tapping into that deeper level, at times, through its influence on discourse, but they may be overlooking how the content of a narrative, even a seeming coherent narrative, is masking an underlying restriction or displacing of immediate experience.

This is useful for understanding why there is the intuitive understanding that the context for language expression matters. Different topics or situations will correlate with an individual's underlying experience in particular ways, but to the extent these connections are located at an implicit level, they will not generally be accessible to narrative analysis. To my knowledge, the attachment literature is unique because it has linked language use of adults, both longitudinally and intergenerationally, to the underlying attachment behaviors of those adults as infants and with their infants, correlating language to action and affect. Given this, attempts to find the mechanisms of healing through narrative that do not take the implicit levels of action and affect into account will encounter difficulties (e.g. Niederhoffer and Pennebaker, 2009). I am arguing that decontexting experience from its narrative surround can, however, more readily reveal implicit assumptions, expectations, and intentions that are restricting attentional flexibility to what is occurring in immediate experience and make it more available for monitoring, reflection, and interpretive analysis.

Thus, coherence of narrative, as such, when determined from the linguistic level, will give rise to the problems narrative psychology has in linking narrative coherence to mental and physical health.

This takes us to the second reason for my critique of narrative psychology.

DOI: 10.1057/9781137300577

5

It's Hard to See through Our Stories

Abstract: *Narrative identity practices assume individuals have access to their experience. A critical question is the extent to which we can see through the filters of past conditioning and socio-cultural conventions, piercing the narrative veil, to access what is happening in immediate experience. Examples where narrative meanings subordinate practice are provided to illustrate the problem and this chapter highlights how Rollo May, the existential-humanistic scholar, and the critical theorist, Walter Benjamin, have addressed the issue.*

Forrest, Kelly. *Moments, Attachment and Formations of Selfhood: Dancing with Now.* Basingstoke: Palgrave Macmillan, 2013. DOI: 10.1057/9781137300577.

 DOI: 10.1057/9781137300577

We have this wonderful capacity to communicate with each other through language. We create and develop concepts as a way to share who we are and how we experience the world. As beings, we all need a place to be, to exist in the world and be affirmed in that existence: individual and society, together. Our language, however, can only express what we are aware of in our experience.

Narrative's foci on context and historicity pulled us out of a partial view of the human, the positivist story, and allowed us back into people's lives. We learned about people's struggles, heard hitherto silenced stories and voices, and have gained a very real understanding of the role that meaning-making plays in our lives. We have seen how story structures experience and identity and how much we cherish coherence and order in ourselves and in the world. But, I am arguing, the pendulum has swung too far to the side of narrative and away from immediate experience. For narrative also has its ghosts, the ghosts of our fears, of disorder, of chaos that binds us to selves and identities, to stories, to narrative based coherence that veils us from the ground of our being, from that which is in our present experience in each moment, and thus from each other.

The critical question is how much of being are we experiencing? To know, we would have to see through our stories, through the "reality" of our conditioning, the implicit assumptions that language assists us to avoid. How hard is it to see through our stories? Is this even possible?

I think it fitting to use language itself as an example, as language also has an implicit assumption on which our interaction with it is based.

Read the following poem, entitled *Suspended in Air*, by Lord Byron (1788–1824).

> I'm not in earth, nor the sun, nor the moon;
> You may search all the sky, I'm not there.
> In the morning and evening, though not at noon,
> you may plainly perceive me, for like a balloon, I am suspended in air.
> Though disease may possess me, and sickness and pain,
> I am never in sorrow nor gloom;
> Though in wit and wisdom, I equally reign,
> I'm the heart of all sin and have long lived in vein,
> Yet, I ne'er to be found in the tomb.

To what is Byron referring? As you are attempting to figure out this riddle, also observe the process you are engaging in to discern the meaning. To figure out to what Byron is referring, we engage in a trial and error process of fitting potential candidate answers to a test of fit to the conditions set forth in the poem, that is, we make claims of meaning, evaluate the claim, discard one claim, and try on another.

There are clues pointing the way, but they are difficult to discern because there is an assumption that is getting in the way, the assumption in our relationship to language. This assumption is as the ground we are standing on and we can't move because we don't know we are standing on it, we don't know it is ground!

How long do you think you could keep going with this process of "figuring out" possible meanings, making and remaking claims? Could it be a long time, perhaps a lifetime?

Let's stop that process now. Words are symbols, they refer to something other than themselves. Thus, when you are attempting to discern to what Byron is referring, this basic assumption is utilized without even thinking about it. The assumption was learned as part of learning to read and it continues to be adaptive in relation to language use. Language use requires this assumption. What Byron has done is remove the assumption!

He has created a poem using language that requires you to go outside of your assumed relation to language to answer the riddle. In other words, he is challenging us to see through a story, the story at the core of our relation to language, the story of meaning.

If you think about the word, "dog," of what do you think? The word refers to, well, it gets hard here because we're using words, but it refers to a real dog, a dog outside the word dog, the one that moves around in all its wiggly particularity when you're about to go for a walk. Byron is asking you not to make that symbolic assumption. He is asking you to eschew this assumption, just for a moment, and allow words to refer back to themselves. Huh! Yeah, that is what happens when an assumption is pointed out. It is so ingrained, that even when it is baldly asserted, it still doesn't compute. If the word dog doesn't refer to your wiggly friend, but instead itself, then all that is left is the word – dog. All that the word dog has that isn't outside of it are what makes up the word, its letters, d-o-g.

The answer to the poem is the letter "i." The letter "i" fits all the conditions, it is literally suspended in a-i-r. Without removing the assumption, the psychological result is as standing in front of a wall, meaning-making foundering under the weight of its own condition. The use of what normally works to figure something out will never work because it is based in a "reality" that both grounds and thwarts the effort. That is why seeing through a story is so hard.

DOI: 10.1057/9781137300577

It is hard and can be painful to see through our own so storied selves. There are clues, however, from those that are pointing toward the assumptions we hold in relations to ourselves and to others, the assumptions that narrating is inadequate to reveal. Some may argue that I am not referring to narrative, that instead, I am speaking more appropriately of character dispositions, those conditioned ways of being in the world that rest beneath narrative, and as such have a separable domain from narrative. This argument, if made, only strengthens the argument herein as it substantiates the schism between words and being.

The existential-humanistic stream in psychology, the stream this project sees itself within, has been pointing since the middle of the last century to the disappearing relationship of words to being and its connection to sources of suffering in our society. I believe it is time now for a renewing of this fertile source both within and outside psychology. Its focus on being speaks directly to those who are calling for the embodiment of discourse, the inclusion of affect and action into theory (e.g. Massumi, 2002).

Rollo May was a psychoanalyst in this tradition. In *Power and Innocence: A Search for the Sources of Violence* (1972), May connects the need to communicate, to share experience, with a person's basic power to be. The communication provides an avenue for a response, an affirmation or signification, to the assertion of being in the world. When being, and thus, self-affirmation and self-assertion are blocked, it can result in compulsivity, neurosis, psychosis, aggression, or violence. The individual and the society take part in violence.

> We often speak of the tendency toward violence as building up *inside* the individual, but it is also a response to outside conditions. The source of violence must be seen in both its internal and external manifestations, a response to a *situation*, which is felt to block off all other ways of response. (May, 1972, p. 44, emphasis in original)

May was speaking at the level of ontology, of being; to feel one's existence as a being is not a matter of nature or nurture, but the root of both, the human being as activity, as an experiencing being, not as a noun, but as a verb, a human be-ing.

Critical social theorists, notably Walter Benjamin and Susan Buck-Morss, point to the narratives in modernity that assail being as be-ing; using concrete images dialectically to reveal paradox, awakening us from story. In this work, there is no distinction between modernity and

DOI: 10.1057/9781137300577

postmodernity, both, as one age, are characterized by trauma, by the ongoing and accumulating shocks to consciousness of the sequelae of imperialism, capitalism, Fascism, and industrialization (Buck-Morss, 1989). Benjamin, through the deliberate fragmented character of his work, tries to awaken us to and from the socio-cultural narratives that source human suffering, that block immediate experiencing behind a veil of meaning (Buck-Morss, 1989, p. 337). He asks us to see the social world through the concrete images and structures of our everyday lives, to see the violent contradictions in which we are living; those very contradictions that our socio-cultural products both house and veil, the contradictions that narratives conceal within the distraction of meaning.

For example, in the urban renewal projects in Paris around 1900, Benjamin saw the reification of the narrative of progress, "with its unmediated identification of technological change with social betterment" (Buck-Morss, p. 92). Using this mythic image, the old Paris was demolished on a massive scale, replaced by "wide boulevards, lined with uniform building facades that seemed to stretch into infinity and punctuated by national monuments" (p. 89).

> The [new] urban "perspectives"... were intended to give the fragmented city an appearance of coherence. In fact the plan, based on a politics of imperial centralization, was a totalitarian aesthetics, in that it caused "'the repression of every individualistic part, every autonomous development'" of the city, creating an artificial city where the Parisian [...] no longer feels at home'" (p. 89–90).

Under the storied veil, the "true goal" of this "strategic beautification" "'was the securing of the city against civil war,'" to "undermin[e] the revolutionary potential of the working class" (p. 90). "'The width of the avenues was to prohibit the erection [of street barricades], and new streets were to provide the shortest routes between the barracks and the working class sections'" (p. 90).

Rollo May (1972), too, saw through the narrative of "growth" as an ethic for betterment. "The illusion that we become good by progressing a little more each day is a doctrine bootlegged from technology and made into a dogma in ethics where it does not fit ... in ethics ... the term *progress* has no place ... Modern [humans are] not ethically superior to Socrates and the Greeks, and although we build buildings differently, we do not make them more beautiful than the Parthenon" (p. 255). Moreover, "it is completely forgotten that joy increases to the extent that the capacity for

DOI: 10.1057/9781137300577

woe does also" (p. 255). You don't just get to keep getting more joyful. He quotes William Blake:

> Man was made for joy and Woe;
> And when this we rightly know
> Thro' the world we safely go,
> Joy & Woe are woven fine,
> A Clothing for the Soul divine. (p. 255)

We are then reminded that each of us has joy and woe and that growth can be both good and evil, but growth for the sake of growth is a cancer. Thus, the truth of human experience reveals the sleight of hand in the narrative of progress that veils the necessary balancing of one element with another, there is joy and woe, growth within bounds.

In the field of trauma narrative studies, the limitations of narrative have been thoughtfully and compassionately interrogated (Caruth, 1995; 1996). It is in this area that the consequences of the foregrounding of coherence and meaning over practice is so horrifically brought to the surface. For the perpetrators, a coherent story of identity, of self – the story of racial superiority – allowed the inhuman treatment of fellow beings. For the survivors, how does one construct a narrative, to integrate incomprehensible experience into meaning structures? At the core of trauma narrative work is the call to listen to the truth of the reality of experience, "the force of its affront to understanding" (p. 154). The study of trauma narrative in the literary field is "responding" to rather than narrating the experience of the trauma survivors. It has not tried to cover anything over with words, for the sake of a linguistic knowing that forsakes the visceral realities of what is going on. Rather, those realities remain in existence, as they remain in human experience. It is a courageous responding.

Rollo May in *The Courage to Create* (1975) explains that courage, in all its forms, requires a centeredness in being, that which enables a movement forward, not without despair, but in spite of despair, because there is an inner commitment. Physical courage requires the capacity to listen with the body, to use the body as a sensitive instrument, as a means of empathy with others. Moral courage comes through a sensitivity to and compassion for human suffering.

> If we let ourselves experience the evil, we will be forced to do something about it. It is a truth, recognizable in all of us, that when we don't want to become involved, when we don't want to confront even the *issue* of whether

> or not we'll come to the aid of someone who is being unjustly treated, we block off our perception, we blind ourselves to the other's suffering, we cut off our empathy with the person needing help. (May, 1975, p. 17, emphasis in original)

Social courage is the courage to risk one's self for meaningful intimacy, the "courage to invest one's self over a period of time in a relationship that will demand increasing openness." Social courage requires that we confront the twin fears, the fear of life and the fear of death. The life fear stops one from living fully, afraid of abandonment; the death fear is the fear of engulfment, that independence will be taken away. There is also creative courage, the courage to create new forms, new structures within which to live, the courage of artists, poets, and saints, each rebelling against the status quo, the powers that be within and without.

So, it is not impossible to see through our stories, but is still hard and, at times, painful. We need words to communicate with ourselves and with others, but these words need to be nourished and vitalized by present centered experience at the level of being.

In narrative research, the shift to small stories is moving in the direction of experience that is "grounded in bodily interactions" and occurs as "embodied talk" (Bamberg, 2011, p. 18). However, the attentional emphasis on claimings and unfolding claimings in narratives in interaction too easily camouflages the constraints on immediate experience based on past conditioning and the positioning grid, the narratives of socio-cultural categorical conventions. Small stories are said to be "social practices for rehearsing, exploring and negotiating the gap between actual and possible, reality and imagination" and "habitual systems for projecting social personas and meanings onto specific locales, which in turn provide interpretive grids for assessing past, present, and future" (Georgakopoulou, 2007, p. 152). The focus is on self as more dynamic and relational, and yet the Moments project data raises important questions. How much of individual experience is shared and how much of experience is even available for identity construction or interactive co-construction?

From the 120 moments collected, 16 per cent had never before been shared. Of the 39 moments deemed most important by the subjects, 13 per cent had not been shared. Of these unshared important moments, 80 per cent were labeled as inconsistent either with one's current view of self or with how one talks about one's self to others. Of the remaining moments, 54 per cent of those that were unshared reported such inconsistency. With the shared moments, less reported inconsistency is found.

DOI: 10.1057/9781137300577

Of the most important moments that were shared, 35 per cent reported a felt inconsistency with self-claims. With the remaining shared moments, 51 per cent reported such an inconsistency.

This data is only suggestive and the percentages are relatively low, but without a focus on unmediated and immediate experience, claims of identity and self are embedded in and influenced by the constraints of past conditioning and socio-cultural conventions, even with the turn to narrative in interaction. This is the reason why conditioning and socio-cultural categorizations are so powerful and destructive. They are used both to validate and invalidate ways of experiencing in the world and can be vigorously and violently defended under threat or perceived threat. The potential for resisting change in one's conditioning and the hegemony of socio-cultural categorizations are, therefore, understandable. They are the ground upon which people claim identity and self.

In *Freedom with Violence: Race, Sexuality, and the US State,* Reddy (2011) argues that non-normative categories of being serve as a foundation of identity for the modern subject and, as such, narrate a landscape in political modernity that delivers freedom only with the counter violence that such freedom necessitates. If one asks, what perpetuates violence? The answer is to look toward identity; in this case, the identity of the nation–state, an identity that deploys violence against some to deliver freedom from violence for others; the contradictions veiled behind the liberal–equalitarian and republican–national narratives, both serving the hegemony of the nation–state's identity. Whether for a nation or an individual, it is time to see through the obfuscatory, regulatory, and hegemonic processes of identity that veil violent contradictions embedded in narratives of myopic coherency.

Niebuhr (1963) understood the destructive potential of socio-cultural categorizations as the bases for interpretation of action, both of our own action and that of others' action upon us. Power structures of domination and subordination are fostered and maintained, while allowing for seeming freedom of changing affiliations and political positioning. In social psychology, social identity theory describes the relationship of group affiliation to self-esteem and the concomitant negative consequences for behavior against out groups resulting from its threat.

The emphasis on self, on narrating "Who am I?" at all levels, thus concretizes fixities of cognitive categories of inclusion and exclusion across the widest range of human experience, with identities constructed and positioned in accord or disaccord with such categorizations. In this

DOI: 10.1057/9781137300577

gridding of experience, self and identity, as other identity constructs, can become little more than effects of imitative performativity (Butler, 1990) produced by the defensive self-regulatory practices of identity coherence with little or no grounding outside the relevant socio-cultural categorizations and past conditioning. The focus on interpretive construction, all the while, maintaining the mind/body dualism, the symbolic, the image, the word separated from the experience of the feared chaos of our so unruly embodiment.

In contrast, the current critique shifts attention toward what is happening in immediate experience and argues that claimings and unfolding claimings of self and identity are problematic as they become the psychological hegemonic tightening threads of thought that constrain and subordinate immediate experience. With these claims of identity and self as a focus of concern, immediate experience will be, of necessity, subordinated to constructed symbolic forms of meaning. You can hear someone say, "This is just who I am." What gets lost is all these claims veil, that which would naturally arise to answer the question, "What is happening?"

DOI: 10.1057/9781137300577

6
What Is Happening?

Abstract: *Drawing from Walter Benjamin's essays on the poet, Charles Baudelaire, this chapter explores the consequences on individual experience due to interactions that are increasingly based on a technological rather than a human agenda. Desensitization, fear, rage, sadness and weariness are addressed in the context of exploring the extent to which the ongoing shocks of living in modernity result in self-regulating routines that replace immediate experience.*

Forrest, Kelly. *Moments, Attachment and Formations of Selfhood: Dancing with Now.* Basingstoke: Palgrave Macmillan, 2013. DOI: 10.1057/9781137300577.

Critical theorists link modernity with trauma. Both are social experiences that reflect loss, violence, and the break up of deeply held truths. The modern subject has to contend with industrialization, rapid technological change, colonial subjugation, postcolonialism, immigration, financial austerity, the atrocities of war, and global terrorism experienced within politicized discourses of contradiction and paradox (e.g. Reddy, 2011). Based on Walter Benjamin's, *The Writer of Modern Life*, the modern subject copes with the ongoing shocks from these conditions through a process of desensitization, by losing the "capacity for experiencing" (Benjamin, 2006, p. 201).

Benjamin's essays highlight the phenomenological experience of an individual – the lyric poet Charles Baudelaire – struggling with the forces of modernity emerging in Paris in the mid-1800s. Although much has changed in the last 150 years, the struggling of the modern subject remains, as if still, Baudelaire is walking, now as ghost, amidst an ever more unresponsive and violently distracted, globalized, and virtualized "Paris."

What is seen walking through the streets of modern life? The gas lamps have long since been extinguished, but the stars and the moon are gone too, replaced not by the glare of the light bulb, but by a consciousness that no longer looks up in awe and wonder. The modern subject does not with bare feet stand on the ground feeling the solidity of the earth, breathing the generosity of trees, and bowing to the awareness of existence and to each other. Such reverence is rendered intoxicant and reserved for the constructions of hand and mind, the tallest building, the thinnest microchip. The bustle of the crowd, still there and grown larger in population, is miniaturized, digitized, and placed in the palm of the hand. The modern identity, numbed to the "unfeeling isolation of each with his private concerns," controls the stimulation of the masses, if only virtually, all turned on and off with a stroke of a key (p. 88).

The nature of that key, fear, the fear of life, the fear of death, the fear of losing one's trace, of disappearing forever into the anonymity of the crowd; these fears too become commodity in the marketplace. Fear is sold along with many things. To make commodity of the phenomenological consequences of commodification is the path of modernity. The price is human experience.

In the urban setting, people, in riding buses and trams, were placed for the first time, in "situations where they had to look at one another for long minutes or even hours without speaking to one another" (p. 69).

DOI: 10.1057/9781137300577

This was, at the time, a "strange" and "unpleasant" situation that created a sense of "uneasiness." Today, a normative asocial quality permeates the public sphere with responsibility for unease shifted to the private realm, an individual coping with stress.

Gone too is any feeling of "brutal indifference" referred to within Friedrich Engels' description of walking amidst the bustle of a London crowd.

> The hundreds and thousands of people from every class and rank crowding past each other – are they not all human beings with the same qualities and powers, and with the same interest in being happy?... And still they crowd by one another as though they had nothing in common, nothing to do with one another, and their only agreement is the tacit one that each keep to his own side of the pavement, so as not to delay the opposing stream of the crowd, while no man thinks to honor another with so much as a glance. The brutal indifference, the unfeeling isolation of each with his private concerns, becomes the more repellant and offensive the more these individuals are crowded together in a limited space. (p. 88)

With the emergence of "crowd," standardized identificatory practices proliferated, houses once named are numbered, photographs capture existence, and with current technological advances, the issue reaches its nadir with identity theft a primary concern. Individuals disappear into type, image, category, and number, each used as a strategy of orientation against a phenomenological ground of the masses. With identity linked to category, the corporation as person becomes a natural entailment.

Benjamin describes some images of modern identity in Baudelaire's poetry and in contemporary literature. For example, there is the flâneur, one who saunters, moving through the masses with charming ambivalence as both a part of and divorced from the crowd as a way to manage the level of stimulation. There is also the amateur detective, who with the hypervigilance of prey expertly discerns the antisocial in the throng. There are the absentminded who "roam[] the... city lost in thought" (p. 99) and the dandies who quickly and nonchalantly react to the vagaries of world markets pleasingly settling conflicts using the trained "art of not pleasing." (p. 125). And, there is the hero.

There are many heroes in modernity. One is the passionate suicide of the laborer who despairs of earning a living in the marketplace. Benjamin describes a small book published in 1841 that "sought to recruit for the

DOI: 10.1057/9781137300577

workers' associations the old corporations of itinerant journeyman which stuck to guild practices" (p. 105). When the author's call was not successful, he took his own life, and in an "open letter invited his companions in misfortune" to do the same (p. 105). Benjamin believes Baudelaire may have viewed "suicide as the only heroic act still available to the *multitudes maladives* of the cities in reactionary times" (p. 105).

On 18 December 2010, Mohamed Bouazizi, a Tunisian street vendor, set himself on fire to protest the confiscation of his wares and his treatment by municipal authorities. His act and later death catalyzed the demonstrations and protests, termed the Arab Spring, across the Middle East and North Africa, resulting in the overthrow of four governments, Tunisia, Egypt, Libya, and Yemen, and sparking unrest in others. In Tunisia, President Zine El Abidine Ben Ali had been in power for 23 years.

According to Benjamin, what typifies the experience of the modern subject is shock. The nature of the shocks are the responses of the human psyche to the interaction with the automated fixities of the machine. It is a technological agenda not an experiential human agenda which drives responses. Benjamin discusses this in terms of action and consequence, "a single abrupt movement of the hand triggers a process of many steps" (p. 190). He mentions the telephone, "where the lifting of receiver had taken the place of the steady movement that used to be required to crank the older models" and the camera, where "the 'snapping' by the photographer"... "a touch of the finger" "gave a posthumous shock" "fix[ing] an event for an unlimited period of time." (p. 190–191)

Optic shocks of this kind occurred from the "advertising pages of a newspaper" and the "traffic of a big city." "Moving through this traffic involves the individual in a series of shocks and collisions. At dangerous intersections, nervous impulses flow through him in rapid succession, like the energy from a battery" (p. 191). Baudelaire describes the experience of shock as "plunging into a reservoir of electric energy" and calls the modern human "a kaleidoscope endowed with consciousness." (p. 191). The "comfort" of the urban, thus, "brings those enjoying it closer to mechanization" (p. 190).

Today, the most striking aspect of these descriptions is the comparative dullness that corresponds to the current experiential corollaries, except perhaps for the occasional incident of road rage. If there is excitement in the use of technology, it is a fascination largely removed from feeling, but observable if one attends to the objects of attention. There is

DOI: 10.1057/9781137300577

the gripping fascination of quick movements, now every 1–2 seconds on the television screen, for making things happen instantaneously with the touch of a key, and for the apparent freedom that accompanies the disconnect between what is and what is preferred that motivates any search.

Are we the audience for whom Baudelaire was writing, those familiar with the "spleen" that "kills interest and receptiveness," for whom "sensual pleasure" is preferred and "willpower and the ability to concentrate are not... strong points?" (p. 170). What remains shocking for the post-modern modern subject? Living amidst ongoing shocks, the body and psyche, as in response to chronic trauma, develop habits of avoidance and preoccupation to protect against further assault.

In this context, self-regulating routine replaces responsivity. In this regard, Benjamin contrasts the training of the factory worker to the practice of handcraft. In practice, the form of the activity is discovered through experience; in contrast, in training, the standardization of activity, the repetition of gesture necessitated by the machine seals-off work from experience. The worker becomes as gambler, each act independent of its predecessor, conditioned to repeat the last act exactly, to coordinate this act "with the uniformly constant movements of an automaton" (p. 191). Both the gambler and wage earner must continually start all over again.

This condition is playing itself out across the globe as savings, pensions, and investments, the security built up over a lifetime of action, swept away, are not to be replenished. The stage is now reset. Action and consequence are divorced within individual experience and socially transposed, the action *of* one is the consequence *for* another. There are no witches anymore; the mixing of "fair is foul, and foul is fair" is removed from the realm of ethics, and becomes instead perceptual, "the permissible reversal of perception" (p. 28). Do we just need to learn not to flinch?

There is something that is being "irretrievably lost" (p. 197). This is set forth by Baudelaire in a poem, entitled *Correspondences*, that begins:

> Nature is a temple whose living pillars
> Sometimes give forth a babel of words;
> Man wends his way through forests of symbols
> Which look at him with their familiar glances.
> Like resounding echoes that blend from afar
> In a somber, profound unity,

DOI: 10.1057/9781137300577

> Vast as the night or as the brightness of day,
> Scents, colors, and sounds respond to one another. (p. 198)

Benjamin describes what Baudelaire meant by correspondences as "experience which seeks to establish itself in crisis-proof form" (p. 198). What is the nature of such experience?

Benjamin states that Baudelaire's idea of correspondences derived largely from Emanual Swedenborg (1688–1772), a Swedish mystic who "envisioned a universal language in which everything outward and visible in nature was a symbol pointing to an inward spiritual cause" (p. 286). For Baudelaire, such correspondences live in ritual as "an encounter with an earlier life" (p. 198). A more contemporary referral to the nature of ritual is in Erik Erikson's, *Identity and the Life Cycle* (1959). Erikson distinguishes between ritualization and ritualism. The ritual of which Baudelaire and Swedenborg describe is ritualization, that which pregnantly carries the sacred, the numinous, with its links to prehistory and community. In contrast, a ritualism is empty, relegated to a going through the motions. At each stage of life, Erikson postulated a crisis of identity that can be characterized along the ritualization/ritualism dimension. From infancy to old age, these are numinous/idolism, judiciousness/legalism, authenticity/impersonation, formality/formalism, ideology/totalism, affiliative/elitism, generativity/authoritism, and integrity/sapientism. It is not difficult to discern on which side the weight of modernity falls.

The experience of shock that characterizes modernity is based on the absence of a natural correspondence: "the expectation aroused by the gaze of the human eye is not fulfilled" (p. 205).

In the mid-1800s, looking into the camera was felt to be "inhuman," even "deadly," as "the camera records our likeness without returning our gaze" (p. 204).

> Inherent in the gaze, however, is the expectation that it will be returned on that which it is bestowed. Where this expectation is met ... there is an experience [*Erfarung*] of the aura in all its fullness. "Perceptibility," as Novalis puts it, "is an attentiveness." (p. 204)

The "experience of the aura" refers to that with which objects can be imbued, such as a cherished momento. The aura "arises from the fact that a response characteristic of human relationships is transposed to the relationship between humans and inanimate or natural objects." "To experience the aura of an object we look at means to invest it with the ability to look back at us" (p. 204).

DOI: 10.1057/9781137300577

Yet, for modern subjectivities, the "response characteristic of human relationships" is not so simple. The eye is "overburdened with protective functions." There are eyes that "look at us with mirrorlike blankness," eyes that "plunge into the fixed stare," "eyes-without-a-gaze," and "eyes that could be said to have lost the ability to look" (p. 204, 205).

The consequence of prolonged interaction with unresponsivity is the "inability to experience," and it is that inability, as May (1972) knew, which constitutes "the true nature of rage" (Benjamin, 2006, p. 200). "The rage explodes in time to the ticking of the seconds that enslaves the melancholy man." (p. 200).

Even in modernity, however, the "chronological reckoning that subordinates duration to regularity…cannot prevent heterogeneous conspicuous fragments [of genuine experience] from remaining within it" (p. 201). What holds the weight of experience is its utter inextricable connection with death. If death is suppressed, experience walks in "borrowed garb" as "ornament" (p.201).

In the shocking, corrosive, and rapid pace conditions of modern times, I am arguing that the narratives of modern social identity are providing, as did the "strategic beautification" of Paris, only the appearance of coherence. As we walk the wide boulevards of our stories, we do not see the underside, that within ourselves that was demolished, is continually being demolished, the immediacy of our experience.

Seen from this perspective, modern social identity is as Baudelaire describes:

> Lost in this base world, jostled by the crowd, I am like a weary man whose eye, looking backward into the depths of the years, sees only disillusion and bitterness, and looking ahead sees only a tempest which contains nothing new, neither instruction nor pain. (p. 209–210)

In this weariness, I see the temporal schism of the little girl in the *Black rocking chair*, lamenting of never being loved and wondering if she will ever feel it in the future. The same schism is there in Baudelaire's "looking backward" and "looking ahead," the one that Ricouer fills with narrative, but the little girl, in the moment, fills with the immediacy of her experience, with felt energy, with love.

And, what of narrative? For the little girl, the narrative of self-judgment linked causally to a disappointed expectation of love articulates an inability to experience the love she knows is now there. For Baudelaire, it expresses his weariness, and for Benjamin, the story goes, he committed

DOI: 10.1057/9781137300577

suicide in expectation of being returned to Nazi hands after fleeing Paris in 1940.

What is happening for the modern subject? I believe it is as for the maker and citizen, a weariness for living in a narrative of lack that is covered by a hope that motivates the endless search for love or justice. Underneath all the distraction is exhaustion, sorrow, and rage.

DOI: 10.1057/9781137300577

7
The Responding Self

Abstract: *In the context of modernity, this chapter suggests the pendulum has swung too far in the direction of narrative meanings. The proposed alternative of working with decontexted experience of moments is discussed as a way to ground the self in the inherent coherence of moments and bring awareness to narrative meanings that constrain and shield immediate experience. In critiquing narrative psychology, a shift of attentional orientation away from answering the question "Who am I?" to that of "What is happening?" is proposed.*

Forrest, Kelly. *Moments, Attachment and Formations of Selfhood: Dancing with Now.* Basingstoke: Palgrave Macmillan, 2013. DOI: 10.1057/9781137300577.

Bringing the critical theory of modernity to psychological experience, I am arguing for decontexted moments of experience as a viable, but neglected alternative methodology for tapping into human experience and for understanding the nature of self and identity. This book argues the pendulum has swung too far in the direction of narrative-based constructions of identity and self which do little more than substitute one organization of selfhood with its own disciplinary understanding. Yet, as theorists of modernity and the attachment literature show, narrative, whether in the telling of a past experience or in a current interactive setting, can too often become a cultural-technological and self-regulatory screen that displaces and shields immediate and unmediated experience in order to quell fears, of life, of death, of chaos. The power of conditioning and socio-cultural conventions pervades narrative. Studying identity practices within a narrative paradigm, as such, in terms of what individuals are doing to organize their worlds is one thing, but to say it offers a privileged entry point into human experience must be qualified by the dangers it presents, the dangers inherent when meanings subordinate practice.

We have seen what narrative has to offer when constructions fail as it does for the boy in *Set for the... snap*, when expectations are not met as for the little girl in the *Black rocking chair*, and when we are subject to laws not our own, as for the *Wonderful sad monkey* and the loss of a baby in the *Question mark* and of a brother in *Everything... lost its context*. The focus on narrative practices as the basis for healing is particularly problematic in this regard because narrative can rigidify and mask deeply conditioned ways of being and knowing that limit access to immediate experience and a more flexible and spontaneous responsivity to self and others in the present. A responsivity that is calling us, as May (1972), to be responsible for our actions, for the effects of our actions, responsible not just to self, but responsible for the effects of our views on others, yes, responsible for the effects of actually being wrong, and responsible to gain awareness of the consequences of our actions, responsible to see and respond to what is happening.

Rather than lamenting some ruined condition, however, this book is fundamentally optimistic in that modernity also holds out the conditions for accessing the grounding of self in action and affect. By studying "moments," decontexted experience that need not be integrated into larger narrative meanings, explicit and implicit attentional "choices" are highlighted and more accessible to awareness. Working with decontexted

DOI: 10.1057/9781137300577

experience on a moment-to-moment basis offers an experientially grounded sense of being that can bring into awareness the constraints of past conditioning and current socio-cultural conventions. In this practice, the inherent coherence of moments is offered as grounding for a healthy self in modern social life. Such grounding, by the nature of the moment-to-moment process, disrupts the rigidifying effects of narrative meanings and quells the existential fears as it slowly, if painfully, liberates experiencing and responsivity in the here and now. It also offers scholars and clinical practitioners an alternative methodology in which to work as a way to enliven deadened or dormant areas in theory and experience. Reconnecting with what naturally arises in experience also has the potential for more successfully transacting selfhoods across individual and socio-cultural differences as it lessens the strength of constricting and divisive narrative overlays and more readily accesses experiential commonalities in affect and action.

The offered approach is not easy, nor is it new. There are many on this path, only some of which are listed or discussed herein. The philosophical and psychological foundations are in the existential-humanistic stream, including Søren Kierkegaard, Paul Tillich, Alfred North Whitehead, Rollo May, Karen Horney, Carl Rogers, James Bugental and all those practicing in the Gestalt phenomenological tradition. Broadly, in social critical theory, I would include Martin Buber, H. Richard Niebuhr, Mikhail Bakhtin, Luce Irigary, Judith Butler, Chandan Reddy, and Brian Massumi. Those who are working to better understand implicit relational knowing are providing needed evidence-based research. Notably, in this regard is the work on attachment, particularly that of John Bowlby, Mary Ainsworth, Mary Main and Erik Hesse as well as the work on infant development and psychotherapy of the Boston Change Process Study Group, including Daniel Stern and Karlen Lyons-Ruth. There are many foregrounding non-linguistic processes centered in the body, a few that stand out are Pat Ogden in trauma psychology, Cathy Caruth and Shosana Felman in literary studies. The emphasis on mindfulness across the social sciences, humanities, and in medicine, incorporating Eastern traditions of meditation and many forms of body process work, are also important contributions (e.g. Kabat-Zinn, 2005).

The approach I am setting forth is inspired by the third image given by Niebuhr (1963). Niebuhr describes this image as the responder. As with be-ing, I am changing this image, moving it from a noun, responder, to the verb, responding. This image necessitates a key shift in attentional

DOI: 10.1057/9781137300577

orientation, from a focus on the question "Who am I?" to that of "What is happening?" Contemporary psychology is a psychology of relational interaction. So we need to move narrative identity practices from an older constructionist model that answers the question "Who am I?" with the teleological question, "What is my goal?" or the deontological question, "What is the law of my life?" to the realities of life beyond these images, the realities of action and interaction, of response and responding, that requires each of us to ask, "What is happening?" and given the totality of interaction, "What is a fitting response?"

The proposed approach moves away from a focus on narrative coherence and claimings of self and identity toward one that foregrounds immediate experience as a foundation for healthy identity and self. I am also removing the image from the Christian frame given it by Niebuhr. I think he would think this is okay. I use the image as a symbol, but not one that divides, the diabolic, but one that bridges across such divides, the symbolic.

There are a number of questions that may arise. What happens to the self, to identity, in this approach? What is immediate experiencing and don't we do that all the time anyway? How does one organize experience for action in the world without creating a fixity of self? What is the role for narrative psychology in such an endeavor?

The self, the core self, that of which Damasio speaks, remains: we will still feel a feeling as my feeling. There will still also be an extended self, but the too cathected emphasis on the narrative self or identity will be defused. The "dilemmatic spaces" (Bamberg, 2011) of sameness or difference with others, or continuity or discontinuity over time will move into the background as self and identity will be more of an emergent structure of living in a moment to moment experience of and responding to what is happening. So too, questions of fit between world and self will recede with a more particularized exploring foregrounded, that of choosing a fitting response from an attentional focus on what is happening in the current moment.

For a definition of the self, I will use that given by Gestalt psychotherapy (Perls, Hefferline, and Goodman, 1951). The self is a "contact boundary at work" forming figures and grounds and responding in any given moment. Regardless of definition, the focus of concern shifts away from self and identity to what is happening in the here and now. Let your identity, your self, arise from your responding. The shift focuses on experiencing, responding, the consequences of responding, the interactive process of contact at the organism/environment boundary.

DOI: 10.1057/9781137300577

With this shift, there will arise the concern that letting go of fixities of self will give rise to chaos. I am not minimizing this concern or the concomitant feelings of fear, anxiety or dread. I am saying that working with this concern and these feelings is the deeper self and identity work that narrative practices shield. Gestalt psychology teaches that feelings of chaos only come when we fail to use spontaneous concentration, following the cycle of experience, from awareness, to sensation, action, contact, and then withdrawal (Perls, Hefferline, and Goodman, 1951; Zinker, 1994). Instead, we interrupt experience, dividing attention, distracted to too many attractors within a ground in which no form is clear, no figure clarifying itself, drawing our attention, interest and excitement. In the mounting anxiety, we want something to hold onto and so we grasp, we grasp at fixities, at categories, at story, at self. This approach, suggests instead a gentle shift of attention, returning to experience of what is happening.

To say unmediated and immediate experiencing is one thing, to distinguish it from what, I would suggest, most of us normally do, is something else. James Bugental's *Psychotherapy 'Isn't' What You Think* (1999) provides an illustration in a therapy context (p. 21).

CLIENT:	I still feel so much sadness – it's crazy to still carry around with me I know – about Jessie being gone. I have mourned enough, for Christ's sake, why can't I let it go.
THERAPIST A:	You're still missing her
THERAPIST B:	(Empathically.) So sad.
THERAPIST C:	How long has she been gone?
THERAPIST D:	Your feelings are at war, the impatience attacking the sadness.

Bugental explains that therapists A and B are drawing attention to the emotion of sadness with B moving toward a deepening of the feeling. Therapist C is looking for information with the possible intention of wanting to evaluate the client's response. It is therapist D, however, who is drawing the client's awareness to what is most present, what is implicitly actual in the living moment, "the pull of mourning and the impatience with its still having such potency" (p. 22). This self-judging aspect linked to the loss is part of the client's experience of loss. Perhaps therapists A and B perceive this as masking the feelings of loss, and as such, they move toward the sadness more directly. However, only the client can know what will arise with the awareness of this link.

If we are talking about unmediated and immediate experiencing, why do we need to have an example? Isn't this process just another

DOI: 10.1057/9781137300577

fixed form? I would offer that the problem is not about fixity as such, it is about awareness of fixities and their consequences. But, we can't be aware of either unless we are aware of our experience of what is happening, to slow down enough to see, hear, and experience in our interpretive meaning-making the figures that are being pulled from a rich ground of being. So, there is a need to increase awareness to discover what stories are organizing experience and what the consequences are within the experience. Without being aware of what is occurring in the moment, Bugental's client cannot even address the impatience he is experiencing or be open to consequences of that impatience.

Thus, this approach embodies the totality of experience, not just one aspect of it, like the sadness. Rather, it allows the impatience, the sadness, and the associative link between the two to exist in awareness. This openness to experience and responding to experience in others is what the second section of this book was illustrating, listening to each moment and responding to the richness held within as best as one can. Becoming aware of what is happening is not the same as constructing a meaning based on logic or plot; what is happening is just what is happening, even if it doesn't make sense. This is why constructing new stories that are more "coherent, accessible, differentiated, and evocative" (Singer, Baddeley, and Frantsve, 2008, p. 117), while potentially fostering more awareness of alternative interpretations, has the danger of substituting one narrative structure for another, bypassing immediate experience.

The stories that are organizing living at the deepest levels, thus, may not be those we think or those we tell because we are so used to the reality of what we think that experiencing something else may be too quickly dismissed, devalued, or otherwise removed from awareness, gone perhaps into an interactive reenactment, a bodily process, a tightness of muscle, or a holding of the breath. It is too easy to think, rethink, tell and retell through habit or fear. The power of the attentional shift away from immediate experience is to equate reality with illusion.

Without the assistance of a master therapist, how can one discern whether experience is mediated by conditioning or socio-cultural conventions? Based on existential-humanistic phenomenology practiced in Gestalt psychotherapy, the approach is to follow what naturally arises in the body and the mind, attend to what is figural, allow it to clarify, then let it go, moving onto the next moment. There is a role for reflection, but it is a present experience of reflecting on past experience. There is only the present moment. Past conditioning and socio-cultural conventions

DOI: 10.1057/9781137300577

will shape experience, but the shift in focus to what is happening shifts awareness and thus the consequences of such fixities. We are now listening to the fixities; they become our teachers, rather than our keepers.

What is the role of narrative psychology in this endeavor? This will depend on the responding of each narrative researcher. The alternative methodology of studying decontexted experience requires trust in human responding as it advocates for fostering awareness of what is happening. A critical shift in attention is needed as narrative identity research focuses on the intersection between the stories we tell and the lives we lead. The approach shifts attention to immediate experience, and in this light, issues once thought important become less relevant. The focus on self and identity, as such, on roles, claims, and positions, are subordinated to a fostering of self/identity practices that encourage awareness of what is happening on the phenomenological level of human experience, on how one responds to that awareness, and the consequences of that responding. It is what I have attempted in my beginning ways in this little book.

The Moments section sought to highlight the experience of moments through responding to each moment as a moment. Of the nine moments presented, three had never been shared with others before the interview, the *Wonderful sad monkey*, *Just trying to reconcile*, and the *Question mark*. Of the remaining moments, only one, *New York cheesecake*, was reported as being typically shared with others, the rest had been shared only with an intimate few. Six of the moments had not been integrated into a larger narrative, but rather remained as an isolated moment of experience unconnected to some larger or smaller narrative, whether shared or not. These were the *Wonderful sad monkey*, *Just trying to reconcile,* the *Black rocking chair, New York cheesecake, Question mark,* and *Everything... lost its context.* In six of the moments, subjects reported an inconsistency with self or with how they talk about self to others. The three moments that were consistent on both were *New York cheesecake, Just pure joy,* and *Whoosh... here I am.* Of the moments presented, six were reported as being the most important moment. These were the *Black rocking chair, New York cheesecake, Whoosh... here I am, Question mark, Everything... lost its context,* and *Just pure joy.*

This descriptive data represents the types of answers that my initial questions going into the Moments project were highlighting. What types of moments will be remembered, will moments be integrated into story, suggesting a unity or multiplicity of self, and will moments

DOI: 10.1057/9781137300577

be shared, indicating socio-cultural influence. Yet, the answers to these questions, do not fully respond to the experiences. The moments were not just put through a critical interpretive filter; rather, I responded to each experience. Someone else would, undoubtedly, have a different response to each moment, but I am arguing that something important occurs in attending and responding to each moment. Moments touch the ground of affect and action; they are deeply intimate and evocative in and of themselves because the moments as moments pierce through, as punctum, protective narrative overlays, and create, at an ontological level, a space for what is.

I also responded to what is happening in narrative psychology by presenting the material in three parts. The first part is in story form, an autoethnographic approach that chronicles my journey in relation to the Moments project. This approach foregrounds episodic memory. The third part is at the semantic level, situating the project within relevant scholarship. The second part foregrounds responding moment to moment. In this part there was no effort taken to create an argument or thread for each moment or one that ran through all the moments, except that of responding to each moment. Each moment was taken on its own and the interpretive exploration sourced what naturally arose in responding to the moment.

The three approaches complement one another just as they overlap in places. Each approach foregrounds certain aspects of the project. Scholarship has built itself primarily on the first and last approaches. This book suggests empirical data and critical social theory can enliven one another, raising new questions and new perspectives at the contact boundary where the theoretical and experiential meet, as momentary companions. Scholarship gains in interdisciplinary accessibility because, while discipline specific language may be used, studying moments grounds the analysis in the common implicit experiential realm of action and affect, offering bridges across domains of knowledge that otherwise are difficult to traverse. I also believe it opens up avenues for the more playful aspects in scholarship (Massumi, 2002). I am speaking of serious play, that openness of exploration allowing room both for and from the creative (Winnicott, 1971). Ethics also plays a critical part in this endeavor. Rollo May and others from the existential-humanistic stream speak to this connection.

Decontexting experience from habitual narratives opens the way for neglected aspects of experience to emerge, gradually awakening

DOI: 10.1057/9781137300577

deeply held socio-cultural and personal expectations, assumptions, and intentions. Coming into awareness of heretofore implicit ways of experiencing can challenge cherished narratives of self and world, as does traveling in a different culture. Awareness of areas of avoidance or distracted preoccupation will be resisted as they are the result of conditioning from whatever source. For individuals, this process can be painful, as expressed by some subjects in the Moments project. In such circumstances, assistance with the healthy regulation of what is arising may be necessary. In a therapeutic context, the alternative approach may be especially beneficial for clients with post-traumatic stress, whether it be from acute or complex trauma histories, as conditioning from trauma is in the service of disconnecting awareness from its grounding in the body and from what is happening. In the context of modernity, however, none of us is exempt from such conditioning. Working with shifting attention to non-traumatic current experience in the moment has the potential to gradually reestablish connection to the body, bringing into awareness self-narratives that veil such experience. We will always construct narratives, but this practice seeks to utilize language in the service of harmonizing mind and body, focusing on listening to current experience, responding to what arises and to the consequences of one's responding. I would note that, as for psychotherapy, scholarship too, isn't what we think, but rather its effects on how we live. This is the testimony and argument made so strongly in critical pedagogy by Paolo Friere (1970/2010), that learning and being are not separate.

These are just some beginning thoughts for steps on this path. What we are talking about here is a difference of what produces relationality and what produces it better. What is being suggested is a refocusing of attention to the "*actual* in the moment experiencing" regardless of the content, be it history, hopes, values, pain or self-judgments (Bugental, 1999, p. 22).

It is easy to look away from experience to meaning; it takes time to even know we are doing it. But, we can see the consequences. Bugental was a master therapist. I am only starting on this path. But, I think that all of us have losses and all of us are mourning and too many of us are impatient, as was Bugental's client, with its continued potency. Awareness and responding are the next steps, awareness of immediate experience, of what is happening, and responding with awareness of the consequences.

We needn't fear chaos; that only comes with distracted attention. There is coherence in the moment with no opposition between remembering

DOI: 10.1057/9781137300577

and living, between past and present experience. Now, with awareness, we have a choice to choose our relationship to what is arising in each moment. The moments are telling us that there is a ground, a ground of be-ing, the ground in each moment, that has a coherence, that has an order, even if we don't understand it or feel it at first. The choice is whether to trust this coherence even if what is happening is not what we would prefer. Niebuhr (1963) agreed with the need for trust. As it was told to me, it is simple... yet difficult.

Altering how one meets each moment in living is not done through understanding, through a new interpretation of the ways we are in the world, through a new story, or even a new image of responding; rather, allowing a space for awareness of how we are choosing to meet each moment is all that is necessary, to experience what is happening and responding to that awareness.

The attachment literature shows that security of attachment is based, not on holding a narrative of self, whether apparently coherent in story or not, but on the ability to flexibly, thus freshly, respond to what is arising in the present moment. It is ironic that security is associated with flexibility and spontaneity, but it is! The attachment literature, if allowed to speak to security and attachment in the broadest sense, draws aside the narrative veil disclosing the individual and intergenerational consequences of holding on to conditioned ways of organizing experience, that is, the self's desire for security. Moments come and go; impermanency is the nature of time, but there is order and coherence in each moment. We partake of change in our being and yet, each of us has areas of fixities that both protect and dull our awareness of immediate experience and responsivity to self and others. Not all fixities are negative all the time, but we need to see and respond to the consequences for ourselves and others of those we are explicitly or implicitly choosing.

There will be pain and suffering. We need to experience this suffering, rather than avoid it. Why? If we keep trying to avoid suffering, the consequence is a lessening of awareness to suffering and a lessening of responding to suffering. So, when there is suffering, we are conditioning ourselves to avoid it, to avoid seeing it, avoid experiencing it, and those consequences play out in a desensitized and divided society. Concomitantly, by not avoiding suffering, we become more sensitive to suffering in ourselves and in others. We will feel more pain, more woe, but we will also feel more joy. We may also become better at accepting and letting go.

DOI: 10.1057/9781137300577

In this process, human experience is foregrounded in the chain of causality. The bottom line is no longer based in a narrative of economic efficiencies, but in the actuality of human experience, in suffering. What is the index of gross domestic suffering?

We will make mistakes because we can only know the effects of an action by its consequences. This little piece of reality is problematic and it is why science is so keen on prediction, but we all know, prediction is just that, and life happens the way it does, regardless of our tireless constructions, interpretations, and planning to the contrary. As my mentor's mentor said, we all need to make plans, just don't count on them.

This approach, responding to what is actual in each moment, as best one can, learning from the past, but not identifying with it, seeing the consequences of following the fixities in our lives, allowing more spontaneity and flexibility for identity and self to emerge out of responding rather than making claims or making things happen for identity, is an approach that needs careful consideration as a way to live amidst the ongoing trauma, loss, and uncertainty that modernity entails.

Allowing room for attending to our unmediated and immediate experiencing without needing to act upon it, judge it, banish it, or make a story out of it, just to observe, to listen, allows room to be, room for responding out of what arises naturally, not reactively to the demands of past conditioning or socio-cultural categorizations. I believe this is at the core of what Niebuhr (1963) was saying as well.

Placing awareness on immediate experience is needed now as the pendulum has swung too far to the side of narrative. Meanings founder when their natural grounding in experience is undercut. What is needed for meaning to regain its footing in modernity is a momentary approach for healthy identity and self, one that foregrounds immediate experience in the context of responding to "What is happening?" In this approach, identity and self are not a focus of construction, co-construction, or positioning; they are emergent phenomena continually becoming through a process of moment-to-moment responding, but subordinated to an awareness of what is happening in immediate experience, being with being, dancing with now.

DOI: 10.1057/9781137300577

References

Ainsworth, M. D. S. (1967). *Infancy in Uganda: Infant Care and the Growth of Love*. Baltimore: Johns Hopkins University Press.

Ainsworth, M. D. S., Blehar, M. C., Waters, E., and Wall, S. (1978). *Patterns of Attachment: Assessed in the Strange Situation and at Home*. Hillsdale, New Jersey.: Lawrence Erlbaum.

Angell, J. W. and Helm, R. M. (1988). *Meaning and Value in Western Thought: A History of Ideas in Western Culture, Volume* II: *the Medieval and Modern Development*. New York: University Press of America.

Aristotle (1965). *de Anima*. New Haven, Connecticut: Yale University Press.

Bakhtin, M. M. (1981). *The Dialogic Imagination: Four Essays*. Austin: University of Texas Press.

Bamberg, M. (1997). Oral versions of personal experience: three decades of narrative analysis. *Journal of Narrative and Life History, 7*, 335–342.

Bamberg, M. (2011). *Who am I*? Narration and its contribution to self and identity. *Theory & Psychology*, 21(1), 3–24.

Barthes, R. (1980). *Camera Lucida*. New York: Hill and Wang.

Benjamin, W. (2006). *The Writer of Modern Life: Essays on Charles Baudelaire*. Cambridge, Massachusetts: Belknap, Harvard University Press.

Boston Change Process Study Group (BCPSG) (2010). *Change in Psychotherapy: A Unifying Paradigm*. New York: W.W. Norton & Company.

DOI: 10.1057/9781137300577

Bowlby, J. (1969/1982). *Attachment and Loss, Vol. i, Attachment* (*2nd ed.*). New York: Basic Books.
Bowlby, J. (1973). *Attachment and Loss, Vol. II, Separation.* New York: Basic Books.
Bowlby, J. (1979). *The Making and Breaking of Affectional Bonds*. New York: Routledge.
Bowlby, J. (1980). *Attachment and Loss, Vol. III, Loss, Sadness and Depression.* New York: Basic Books.
Bruner, J. (1986). *Actual Minds: Possible Worlds.* Cambridge, Massachusetts: Harvard University Press.
Buber, M. (1992). *On Intersubjectivity and Cultural Creativity.* S.N. Eisenstadt (ed.). Chicago: University of Chicago Press.
Buck-Morss, S. (1989). *The Dialectics of Seeing: Walter Benjamin and the Arcades Project.* Cambridge, Massachusetts: MIT Press.
Bugental, James F. T. (1999). *Psychotherapy "Isn't" What You Think: Bringing Psychotherapeutic Engagement into the Living Moment.* Pheonix: Zieg Tucker & Co.
Burke, K. (1952). *A Rhetoric of Motives.* New York: Prentice-Hall.
Butler, J. (1990). *Gender Trouble: Feminism and the Subversion of Identity.* New York: Routledge.
Calkins, S. (2004). Early attachment processes and the development of emotional self-regulation. In R. Baumeister and K.D. Vohs (eds) *Handbook of Self-Regulation: Research, Theory, and Applications.* New York: Guilford Press, pp. 324–339.
Carr, D. (1986). *Time, Narrative, and History.* Bloomington: Indiana University Press.
Caruth, C. (ed.) (1995). *Trauma: Explorations in Memory.* Maryland: Johns Hopkins University Press.
Caruth, C. (1996). *Unclaimed Experience: Trauma, Narrative, and History.* Maryland: Johns Hopkins University Press.
Cassidy, J. and Shaver, P. R. (eds) (2008). *Handbook of Attachment: Theory, Research, and Clinical Applications* (*2nd ed.*). New York: Guilford Press.
Damasio, A. (1999). *The Feeling of What Happens: Body and Emotion in the Making of Consciousness.* New York: Harcourt.
D'Cruz, P. (2003). Moments of truth: the experience of wives in HIV/AIDS affected nuclear households in Mumbai, *Journal of Comparative Family Studies*, 34(2), 255–281.
Donnelly, S. M. and Michael, N. (2006). Experience of the moment of death at home, *Mortality,* 11(4), 352–367.

Dozier, M. and Kobak, R. (1992). Psychophysiology in attachment interviews: converging evidence for deactivating strategies. *Child Development*, 63(6), 1473–1480.

Elliott, R., James, E., Reimschuessel, C., Cislo, D., and Sack, N. (1985). Significant events and the analysis of immediate therapeutic impacts. *Psychotherapy*, 22, 620–630.

Erikson, E. H. (1959). *Identity and the Life Cycle*. New York: International Universities Press.

Erikson, E. H. (1963). *Childhood and Society (2nd ed.)*. New York: Norton.

Fonagy, P. and Target, M. (2002). Early intervention and the development of self-regulation. *The Psychoanalytic Inquiry*, 22, 307–335.

Ford, D. (2007). *The Search for Meaning*. Los Angeles: University of California Press.

Friere, P. (1970/2010). *Pedagogy of the Oppressed*. New York: Continuum.

Geertz, C. (1973). *The Interpretation of Cultures*. New York: Basic Books.

Georgakopoulou, A. (2007). *Small Stories, Interaction and Identities*. Amsterdam: John Benjamins Publishing Company.

George, C., Kaplan, N. and Main, M. (1996). Adult attachment interview. Unpublished manuscript, Department of Psychology, University of California, Berkeley (3rd ed.).

Gergen, K. J. and Gergen, M. M. (1986). Narrative form and the construction of psychological science. In T.R. Sarbin (ed.) *Narrative Psychology: The Storied Nature of Human Conduct*. New York: Praeger, pp. 22–44.

Giddens, A. (1991). *Modernity and Self-Identity: Self and Society in the Late Modern Age*. Stanford, California: Stanford University Press.

Helmeke, K. and Sprenkle, D. (2000). Clients' perceptions of pivotal moments in couples therapy: a qualitative study of change in therapy. *Journal of Marital and Family Therapy*, 26(4), 469–483.

Henretty, J. R., Levitt, H. M. and Mathews, S. (2008). Clients' experiences of moments of sadness in psychotherapy: a grounded theory analysis. *Psychotherapy Research*, 18(3), 243–255.

Herman, J. L. (1992). *Trauma and Recovery: The Aftermath of Violence – From Domestic Abuse to Political Terror*. New York: Basic Books.

Hermans, H. J. M. (1996). Voicing the self: from information processing to dialogical exchange. *Psychological Bulletin*, 119, 31–50.

Hermans, H. J. M. (2001). The dialogical self: toward a theory of personal and cultural positioning. *Culture & Psychology*, 7(3), 243–281.

DOI: 10.1057/9781137300577

Hermans, H. J. M., Kempen, H. J. G., and Van Loon, R. J. P. (1992). The dialogical self: beyond individualism and rationalism. *American Psychologist*, 47, 23–33.

Hesse, E. (1999). The adult attachment interview: historical and current perspectives. In J. Cassidy and P. R. Shaver (eds) *Handbook of Attachment: Theory, Research, and Clinical Applications*. New York: Guilford Press, pp. 395–433.

Hesse, E. and Main, M. (2000). Disorganized infant, child, and adult attachment: collapse in behavioral and attentional strategies. *Journal of Psychoanalytic Association*, 48(4), 1097–1127.

Hesse, E., and Main, M. (2006). Frightened, threatening and dissociative parental behavior in low-risk samples: description, discussion and interpretations. *Development and Psychopathology*, 18, 309–343.

Irigary, L. (2008). *Sharing the World*. New York: Continuum.

James, W. (1890/1963). *Psychology*. New York: Fawcett.

Kabat-Zinn, J. (2005). *Full Catastrophe Living: Using the Wisdom of Your Body and Mind to Face Stress, Pain, and Illness*. New York: Delta.

Karen, R. (1998). *Becoming Attached: First Relationships and How They Shape Our Capacity to Love*. New York: Oxford University Press.

Kelly, G. A. (1955). *The Psychology of Personal Constructs, Vols. 1 and 2*. New York: Norton.

Kernberg, O. F. (1976). *Object Relations Theory and Clinical Psychoanalysis*. New York: Aronson.

Kline, M. (1980). *Mathematics: The Loss of Certainty*. New York: Oxford University Press.

Kohut, H. (1971). *The Analysis of Self*. New York: International Universities Press.

Kohut, H. (1977). *The Restoration of the Self*. New York: International Universities Press.

Kuhn, T. S. (1962). *The Structure of Scientific Revolutions*. Chicago: University of Chicago Press.

Labov, W. (1972). *Language in the Inner City: Studies in the Black English Vernacular*. Philadelphia: University of Pennsylvania Press.

Labov, W. and Waletzky, J. (1967). Narrative analysis: oral versions of personal experience. In J. Helm (ed.), *Essays on the Verbal and Visual Arts*. Seattle: American Ethnological Society/University of Washington Press, pp. 12–44.

DOI: 10.1057/9781137300577

Longhurst, L. (2006). The "aha" moment in co-active coaching and its effects on belief and behavioral changes. *International Journal of Evidence Based Coaching and Mentoring*, 4(2), 61–73.

Lyons-Ruth, K. (1999). The two-person unconscious: intersubjective dialogue, enactive relational representation, and the emergence of new forms of relational organization. *Psychoanalytic Inquiry*, 19(4), 576–617.

Mahler, M. S. (1963). Thoughts about development and individuation. *Psychoanalytic Study of the Child*, 18, 307–324.

Mahler, M. S. (1967). On human symbiosis and the vicissitudes of individuation. *Journal of the American Psychoanalytic Association*, 15, 740–763.

Main, M. (2000). The organized categories of infant, child, and adult attachment: flexible vs. inflexible attention under attachment-related stress. *Journal of the American Psychoanalytic Association*, 48(4), 1055–1096.

Main, M., Goldwyn, R., and Hesse, E. (2003). Adult attachment scoring and classification systems. Unpublished manuscript, Department of Psychology, University of California, Berkeley.

Main, M, Hesse, E., and Kaplan, N. (2005). Predictability of attachment behavior at 1, 6 and 19 years of age. In K. E. Grossmann, and E. Waters (eds) *Attachment from Infancy to Adulthood: the Major Longitudinal Studies*. New York: Guilford Press, pp. 245–304.

Main, M., Kaplan, N., and Cassidy, J. (1985). Security in infancy, childhood, and adulthood: a move to the level of representation. In I. Bretherton and E. Waters (eds) Growing points of attachment theory and research. *Monographs of the Society for Research in Child Development*, 50(1–2, Serial No. 209), pp. 66–104.

Main, M. and Weston, D. R. (1982). Avoidance of the attachment figure in infancy: descriptions and interpretations. In C. M. Parkes and J. Stevenson-Hinde (eds) *The Place of Attachment in Human Behavior*. New York: Basic Books.

Massumi, B. (2002). *Parables for the Virtual: Movement, Affect, Sensation*. North Carolina: Duke University Press.

May, R. (1972). *Power and Innocence: A Search for the Sources of Violence*. New York: Norton.

May, R. (1975). *The Courage to Create*. New York: W. W. Norton & Company.

May, R. (1991). *The Cry for Myth*. New York: W. W. Norton & Company.

DOI: 10.1057/9781137300577

McAdams, D. (1985). *Power, Intimacy, and the Life Story: Personological Inquiries into Identity.* New York: Guilford Press.

McAdams, D. (1993). *The Stories We Live by: Personal Myths and the Making of the Self.* New York: Guilford Press.

McAdams, D., Josselson, R., and Lieblich, A. (2006). *Identity and Story: Creating Self in Narrative.* Washington. D.C.: American Psychological Association.

McGaugh, J. L. (2003). *Memory and Emotion: the Making of Lasting Memories.* New York: Columbia University Press.

Mead, G. H. (1934). *Mind, Self and Society.* Chicago: University of Chicago Press.

Meltzoff, A. and Moore, M. K. (1977). Imitation of facial and manual gestures by human neonates. *Science,* 198, pp. 75–78.

Merleau-Ponty, M. (1964). *Primacy of Perception.* W. Cobb (Translator). Evanston, Illonois: Northwestern University Press.

Nagel. T. (1974). What is it like to be a bat?, *Philosophical Review,* LXXXIII, pp. 435–450.

Niebuhr, H. R. (1963). *The Responsible Self: An Essay in Christian Moral Philosophy.* New York: Harper & Row.

Niederhoffer, K. G. and Pennebaker, J. (2009). Sharing one's story: on the benefits of writing or talking about emotional experience. In S. Lopez (ed.), *Oxford Handbook of Positive Psychology* (*2nd ed.*). New York: Oxford University Press, pp. 621–632,.

Ochs, E. and Capps, L. (2001). *Living Narrative.* Cambridge, Massachusetts: Harvard University Press.

Peirce, C. S. (1955). *Philosophical Writings of Peirce.* J. Buchler (ed). New York: Dover Publications.

Perls, F., Hefferline, R. F., and Goodman, P. (1951). *Gestalt Therapy: Excitement and Growth in the Human Personality.* New York: Dell Publishing.

Piaget, J. (1954). *The Construction of Reality in the Young Child.* New York: Basic Books.

Pillemer, D. (1998). *Momentous Events, Vivid Memories.* Cambridge, Massachusetts: Harvard University Press.

Pillemer, D. (2003). Directive functions of autobiographical memory: the guiding power of the specific episode. *Memory,* 11(2), 193–202.

Ramírez-Esparaza, N. and Pennebaker, J. (2006). Do good stories produce good health: exploring words, language, and culture. *Narrative Inquiry,* 16(1), p. 211–219.

Reddy, C. (2011). *Freedom with Violence: Race, Sexuality, and the US State.* Durham: Duke University Press.

Reps, P. and Senzaki, N. (1957/1985). *Zen Flesh, Zen Bones:* a *Collection of Zen and Pre-Zen Writings.* Vermont: Tuttle Publishing.

Rhodes, R. H., Hill, C. E., Thompson, B. J., and Elliott, R. (1994). Client retrospective recall of resolved and unresolved misunderstanding events. *Journal of Counseling Psychology,* 41, 473–483.

Ricouer, P. (1990a). *Time and Narrative, Vol. 1.* Chicago: University of Chicago Press.

Ricouer, P. (1990b). *Time and Narrative, Vol. 3.* Chicago: University of Chicago Press.

Sacks, O. (1970/1987). *The Man Who Mistook His Wife for a Hat and Other Clinical Tales.* New York: Harper & Row.

Salvatore, G., Conti, L., Fiore, D., Carcione, A., Dimaggio, G., and Semerari, A. (2006). Disorganized narratives: problems in treatment and therapist intervention hierarchy. *Journal of Constructivist Psychology,* 19, 191–207.

Sarbin, T. R. (1986). The narrative as a root metaphor for psychology. In T.R. Sarbin (ed.), *Narrative Psychology: the Storied Nature of Human Conduct.* New York: Praeger, pp. 3–21.

Schoppmann, S., Schröck, R., and Schnepp, W. (2007). "Then I just showed her my arms..." bodily sensations in moments of alienation related to self-injurious behavior: a hermeneutic phenomenological study. *Journal of Psychiatric and Mental Health Nursing,* 14(6), 587–597.

Schore, A. N. (1994). *Affect Regulation and the Origin of the Self: the Neurobiology of Emotional Development.* Hillsdale, New Jersey: Erlbaum.

Schore, A. N. (1996). The experience-dependent maturation of a regulatory system in the orbital prefrontal cortex and the origin of developmental psychopathology. *Development and Psychopathology,* 8, 59–87.

Siegel, D. J. (1999). *The Developing Mind: How Relationships and the Brain Interact to Shape Who We Are.* New York: Guilford Press.

Singer, J. A., Baddeley, J. and Frantsve, L. (2008). Supervision of narrative-based psychotherapy. In A. K. Hess, K. D. Hess, and T. H. Hess (eds) *Psychotherapy Supervision: Theory, Research, and Practice* (*2nd ed.*). Hoboken: John Wiley & Sons.

Smith, B. and Sparkes, A. C. (2008). Contrasting perspectives on narrating selves and identities: an invitation to dialogue. *Qualitative Research,* 8(1), 5–35.

DOI: 10.1057/9781137300577

Spangler, G., and Grossman, K. (1999). Individual and physiological correlates of attachment disorganization in infancy. In J. Solomon and C. George (eds) *Attachment Disorganization*, pp. 95–124. New York: Guilford.

Spence, D. P (1982). *Narrative Truth and Historical Truth: Meaning and Interpretation in Psychoanalysis.* New York: W. W. Norton & Company.

Sroufe, L. A. and Waters, E. (1977). Attachment as an organizational construct. *Child Development,* 48, 1184–1189.

Sroufe, L. A., Egeland, B., Carlson, E. A., and Collins, W. A. (2005). *The Development of the Person: the Minnesota Study of Risk and Adaptation from Birth to Adulthood.* New York: Guilford Press.

Stern, D. (2004). *The Present Moment in Psychotherapy and Everyday Life.* New York: Norton.

Taylor, J. B. (2009). *My Stroke of Insight: A Brain Scientist's Personal Journey.* New York: Plume.

The Random House Dictionary of the English Language (RHDEL) (1966). J. Stein and L. Urdang, (eds). Random House: New York.

Tronick, E. Z. (1989). Emotions and emotional communication in infants. *American Psychologist,* 44(2), 112–119.

Tronick, E. Z., Als, H., Adamson, L., Wise, S., and Brazelton, T. B. (1978). The infant's response to entrapment between contradictory messages in face-to-face interaction. *Journal of American Academy of Child and Adolescent Psychiatry,* 17, 1–13.

Vygotsky, L. (1962). *Thought and Language.* New York: Wiley.

Watson, K. C. and Rennie, D. L. (1994). Qualitative analysis of clients' subjective experience of significant moments during the exploration of problematic reactions. *Journal of Counseling Psychology,* 41, 500–509.

Webster's II New Riverside Dictionary (1984). Boston: Houghton Mifflin.

Winnicott, D. W. (1971). *Playing and Reality.* New York: Routledge.

Zinker, J. C. (1994). *In Search of Good Form: Gestalt Therapy with Couples and Families.* San Francisco: Jossey-Bass.

DOI: 10.1057/9781137300577

Index

DOI: 10.1057/9781137300577

DOI: 10.1057/9781137300577

DOI: 10.1057/9781137300577

DOI: 10.1057/9781137300577

DOI: 10.1057/9781137300577

Lightning Source UK Ltd.
Milton Keynes UK
UKOW041552311012

201376UK00001BI/1/P

9 781137 300560